LEPPM

Critical Thinking in Psychology

Cognitive Psychology

Critical Thinking in Psychology – titles in the series

Critical Thinking in Psychology

Cognitive Psychology

Matthew Coxon

Series Editor: Dominic Upton

SAGE | **m** LearningMatters

Los Angeles | London | New Delhi
Singapore | Washington DC

www.learningmatters.co.uk

Los Angeles | London | New Delhi
Singapore | Washington DC

www.learningmatters.co.uk

Learning Matters
An imprint of SAGE Publications Ltd
1 Oliver's Yard
55 City Road
London EC1Y 1SP

SAGE Publications Inc.
2455 Teller Road
Thousand Oaks, California 91320

SAGE Publications India Pvt Ltd
B 1/I 1 Mohan Cooperative Industrial Area
Mathura Road
New Delhi 110 044

SAGE Publications Asia-Pacific Pte Ltd
3 Church Street
#10-04 Samsung Hub
Singapore 049483

Editor: Luke Block
Production controller: Chris Marke
Project management: Diana Chambers
Marketing manager: Zoe Seaton
Copy-editor: Amanda Crook
Cover design: Toucan Design
Typeset by: Kelly Winter
Printed and bound in Great Britain by:
    MPG Books Group

Library of Congress Control Number: 2011945608

British Library Cataloguing in Publication data

A catalogue record for this book is available from
the British Library

ISBN 978 0 86725 522 8

This book is also available in the following formats:

Adobe ebook   ISBN 978 0 85725 671 3
EPUB ebook   ISBN 978 0 85725 670 6
Kindle   ISBN 978 0 85725 672 0

MIX
Paper from
responsible sources
FSC
www.fsc.org   FSC® C018575

For my beautiful wife Caroline

Contents

Series editor's introduction

Studying psychology at degree level

Being a student of psychology is an exciting experience – the study of mind and behaviour is a fascinating and sprawling journey of discovery. Yet studying psychology at degree level brings with it new experiences, new skills and knowledge. This book, one in a comprehensive new series, brings you this psychological knowledge, but importantly brings with it directions and guidance on the skills and experiences you should also be developing during your studies.

Psychology is a growing discipline – in scope, in breadth and in numbers. It is one of the fastest growing subjects to study at GCSE and A level, and the number of students studying the subject at university has grown considerably over the past decade. Indeed, psychology is now one of the most popular subjects in UK higher education, with the most recent data suggesting that there are some 45,000 full-time students currently enrolled on such programmes (compiled from Higher Education Statistics Agency (HESA) statistics available at www.HESA.ac.uk) and it is likely that this number has not yet peaked.

The popularity of psychology is related to a number of reasons, not the least of which is its scope and its breadth – psychology is a sprawling discipline that seeks to analyse the human mind and behaviour, which is fascinating in its own right. Furthermore, psychology aims to develop other skills – numeracy, communication and critical analysis, to name but a few. For these reasons, many employers seek out psychology graduates – they bring a whole host of skills to the workplace and to any activities they may be involved in. This book brings together the knowledge base associated with psychology along with these critical skills. By reading this book, and engaging with the exercises, you will develop these skills and, in this way, will do two things: excel in your studies and your assessments; and put yourself at the front of the queue of psychology graduates when it comes to demonstrating these skills to potential employers.

Developing higher level skills

Only about 15–20 per cent of psychology graduates end up working as professional psychologists. The subject is a useful platform for many other careers because of the skills it helps you to develop. It is useful to employers because of its subject-specific skills – knowing how people act is pertinent in almost any job and is particularly relevant to those that involve working directly with people. Psychology also develops a number of generic and transferable skills that are both essential to effective undergraduate study and valuable to employers. These include higher-level intellectual skills, such as critical and creative thinking, reflection, evaluation and analysis, and other skills such as communication, problem solving, understanding and using data, decision making, organisa-tional skills, teamworking and IT skills.

The Quality Assurance Agency in Higher Education (QAA) subject benchmarks for psychology (www.qaa.ac.uk/Publications/InformationAndGuidance/Pages/Subject-benchmark-statement-Psychology.aspx), which set out the expectations of a psychology degree programme, highlight the sorts of skills that your degree should equip you with. The British Psychological Society (BPS), which accredits your degree course, acknowledges that graduate employability is an important area of focus for universities and expects that opportunities for skills development should be well embedded within your programme of study. Indeed, this is a major focus of your study – interesting as psychology is, you will need and want employment at the end of your degree.

The activities in this book have been designed to help you build the underpinning skills that you need in order to become independent and lifelong learners, and to meet the relevant requirements of your programme of study, the QAA benchmarks and the needs of you and your potential employer.

Many students find it a challenge to develop these skills, often learning them out of context of their study of the core knowledge domains of psychology. The activities in this book aim to help you to learn these skills at the same time as developing your core psychology knowledge, giving you opportunities continuously to practise skills so that they become second nature to you. The tasks provide guidance on what the skill is, how to develop basic competence in it and how to progress to further expertise. At the same time, development of these skills will enable you to better understand and retain the core content of your course – being able to evaluate, analyse and interpret content is the key to deepening understanding.

The skills that the activities in this book will help you to develop are as presented in Table 0.1.

Table 0.1: Skills developed in this book

Generic skills	Transferable skills
• critical and creative thinking	• communication: oral, visual and written
• reflection	• problem solving
• analysing and evaluating	• understanding and using data
	• decision making
	• organisational skills
	• teamwork
	• information technology
	• independent learning

In addition to review and essay questions, each chapter in this book will contain novel learning activities. Your responses will be guided through these activities and you will then be able to apply these skills within the context of cognitive psychology.

Features in this book

At the start of each chapter there will be **learning outcomes**. These are a set of bullet points that highlight the outcomes you should achieve – both skills and knowledge – if you read and engage with the chapter. This will mean at the outset of the chapter that we try to orientate you, the reader, and demonstrate the relevance of the topic.

We have also included learning features throughout the individual chapters in order to demonstrate key points and promote your learning.

- **Bulleted lists** are used within the chapter to convey key content messages.

- **Case studies** are included as part of a critical thinking activity.

- **Tasks** are a series of short review questions on the topic that will help you assess yourself and your current level of knowledge – use these to see if you can move on or whether you need to re-read and review the material.

- **Critical thinking activities** allow for the review of the text by encouraging key critical and creative thinking of the psychology material presented, and provide development of the generic skills. Each of these activities is followed by a **Critical thinking review**, which unpicks the activity for you, showing how it should have been tackled, the main skill it develops and other skills you may have used in completing the activity.

- **Skill builder activities** use the psychology material presented in the text but will be focused on one particular transferable skill as outlined in Table 0.1. Each of these activities is followed by a **Skill builder review**, which may provide further hints and which makes explicit the skills it helps to develop and the benefits of completing the activity.

At the end of the chapter there will also be some pedagogic features that you will find useful in developing your abilities.

- **Assignments**: In order to assess your awareness and understanding of the topic, we have also produced a series of questions for you to discuss and debate with your colleagues. You can also use these questions as revision materials.

- **Summary: what you have learned**: At the end of each chapter we present a summary of the chapter as a series of bullet points. We hope that these will match the learning outcomes presented at the outset of the chapter.

- **Further reading**: We have included items that will provide additional information – some of these are in journals and some are full texts. For each we have provided the rationale for suggesting the additional reading and we hope that these will direct you accordingly.

- **Glossary** entries are highlighted in bold in the text on their first appearance in a chapter.

- Finally, there is a full set of **references** to support all of the material presented in this text.

We hope you enjoy this text, which is part of a series of textbooks covering the complete knowledge base of psychology.

Professor Dominic Upton
February 2012

Chapter 1

Introduction to cognitive psychology

Learning outcomes

By the end of this chapter you should:

- *be able to describe the key features of **cognitive psychology**;*
- *be able to discuss different methods used to study **cognition**;*
- *be able to analyse whether a claim is scientific;*
- *be able to reflect upon your own assumptions about science, and use information technology to learn about new cognitive research.*

Introduction

There were two main aims in writing this book. The first was to inform you about the many exciting research findings and theories that have developed within the broad field of study known as 'cognitive psychology' – a world that, in my opinion, is currently as incredibly diverse, stimulating and exciting now as it was at its first inception (if not more so). The second aim was to help you develop your critical thinking skills. These are vital not only when you are studying but also for both your work life and your life in general. Who wants to be a passive observer of the world that believes everything that they are told? Definitely not me, and hopefully not you. By spending time developing critical thinking skills, the world should begin to take on a whole new light. Throughout the chapters there are therefore tasks, assignments and general food for thought. These aren't here just to fill the pages, so please make time for them because learning and developing as a person involves more than just reading.

So this book will introduce you to a fascinating area of science and will help you develop into a critical thinker – an ambitious task but not one that is beyond us. Let's begin with a question that may be at the front of your mind (wherever that is): What is cognitive psychology?

What is cognitive psychology?

Let's start with a simple definition and build up from there: cognitive psychology is the scientific study of the **mind**. More specifically, it is the scientific study of the mind as an information processor. This is an important definition because it guides several things: the types of **theories** that are developed; the topics that are investigated; the research questions that are asked; the methods that are used; and the conclusions that are reached (so just about everything). As a definition it is not without controversy, and different psychologists might subscribe to it in different ways or to different extents. When you are first learning about the discipline it is a useful definition to help you understand the many varied theories and ideas that belong to cognitive psychology and what ties them together. For the rest of this section we will explore what this means in terms of three aspects:

- areas of interest;

- research and methods;

- philosophy and assumptions.

Areas of interest

So cognitive psychology is the scientific study of the mind. This means that cognitive psychologists may be interested in anything that involves the mind. It really doesn't take long to work out this is quite a lot of things to study. In reality, then, there are some topics that have received relatively little attention while a significant number of other topics have resulted in substantial amounts of excellent research. We'll focus upon the six key areas that the British Psychological Society (BPS) considers important when studying this subject at undergraduate level. These demonstrate the broadness and possibilities of cognitive psychology and are an excellent starting point. For our purposes, then, cognitive psychology will involve the studying of:

- thinking and reasoning;

- learning and memory;

- language;

- perception;

- attention;

- consciousness.

Throughout this book we will look at the psychology of making decisions; solving problems; remembering; forgetting; speaking; reading; writing; perceiving; recognising; focusing attention; and dividing attention – to name but a few.

As you learn more about cognitive psychology you will find it has wide links with many other research areas. The term 'cognitive' is often attached to many areas of psychology, and science more widely, to reflect the integration of the philosophy and methods of cognitive psychology within different disciplines. For example, you may hear of cognitive neuroscience, cognitive science, cognitive therapy, cognitive behavioural therapy, developmental cognitive neuroscience, animal cognition, and social cognition. These are all diverse disciplines and are therefore beyond the reach of this book. However, in the last chapter of this book I will introduce you to **cognitive neuropsychology**, a branch of cognitive psychology that investigates the effects of brain injury and other brain damage, and looks to see what we can learn from these about the processes of the mind.

Research and methods

The types of research questions people ask, and the methods used to answer them, are as diverse as the areas studied. There are some key principles that underpin much of this research work, and a few key methods that have been used lots across the years. These specific methods will be introduced in more detail later in this chapter; at this point, it is important to know that cognitive psychologists rely heavily on the **scientific method**.

The scientific method requires that ideas and theories are developed on the basis of *evidence* that has been directly observed, and can be measured. This involves generating ideas or explanations for things (**hypotheses**), devising tests for these hypotheses, gathering directly observable and measurable evidence, and then deciding if the evidence supports the hypothesis (whether the hypothesis passed its test). These hypotheses let people develop or make judgements about statements or sets of statements that we know as theories. New and changed theories can then be used to make new hypotheses. This process of theory development through the generation of hypotheses, and collection of evidence, is central to understanding how cognitive psychology develops and supports its ideas. If it isn't clear in your head then you may want to re-read this paragraph before going any further. This process of hypothesis generation and testing underpins almost everything a cognitive psychologist does.

Philosophy and assumptions

To study something within any branch of science, or social science, it is important to have an idea about the philosophy and assumptions of that area. Researchers and theorists will have certain beliefs about the world and how it works that have large implications for the questions they ask, the things that they do, and the conclusions they come to. In any area these beliefs may be incredibly diverse, and they may not always be obvious, or completely shared by people who work in that field. Nevertheless, it is still possible to identify particular beliefs that in general define a particular area. For cognitive psychology, the main philosophy is that the human mind can be understood as an information processor, and this is something that we can make discoveries about through careful study and experimentation in line with the general scientific method. The main assumptions of cognitive psychology are therefore grounded in how the mind works, and how it can be studied. This comes full circle to our original definition: cognitive psychology is the scientific study of the mind as an information processor.

Task — In your own words, summarise what defines cognitive psychology. Compare these to your own beliefs. Do you believe that the assumptions and philosophy are correct? Do you believe the methods are appropriate? Do you feel strongly about this at the moment? Your thoughts and views on what defines cognitive psychology will hopefully change as you work through this book, so this is a task that is worth repeating a number of times: what you believe may change; or what you understand by cognitive psychology may change.

You have begun to learn about cognitive psychology at a surface level: the types of topics that are investigated; the ideas behind the method; and the beliefs behind studying the mind in this way. These ideas are presented here as generally agreed upon but it hasn't always been that way. To understand them a bit better it is useful to know how they have developed. At points in this book we will look at the history of an idea so you can learn about it more effectively. What better way to start, then, than with the origins of cognitive psychology.

Origins of cognitive psychology

The study of the mind has a long history going back to (at least) the ancient world, yet the *scientific* study of the mind has a much shorter history. It is difficult to pick an exact year in which a change began, yet many people agree that the founding of the first psychological laboratory in Germany in 1879 was a very important point in time. Founded by Wilhelm Wundt, the laboratory was concerned with moving away from philosophy, and moving towards measuring more **objective** and **empirical** observations under the banner of psychology?

Cognitive revolution

While the establishment of the first psychological laboratory is clearly important, perhaps the most significant period of time was the mid-to-late 1950s and early 1960s. The events from that period, and how they have shaped modern-day psychology, are often called the **cognitive revolution**.

During this time period prominent theories began to emerge that had a common basis: they addressed questions about the mind through scientific observation; and the theories that were constructed considered the mind a complex information processor. We can use the more specific topic of memory as an example. In 1956 a key paper was published by George Miller titled 'The magic number seven, plus or minus two' in which Miller suggested that the limits of short-term memory could be extended by processing information in larger groups (known as chunking); Peterson and Peterson, in 1959, used observations on forgetting nonsense syllables to propose separate information-processing stages in short-term memory; while in 1960, Sperling demonstrated the existence of a very transitory memory that held information for a short period of time, and theorised a set of processing stages associated with this. All of these research articles are now regarded as classics in this field, and all came from a specific period in time when these types of theory were first being talked about and written about. You will learn about how these early theories have influenced current thinking in later chapters.

Part of the development of cognitive psychology as a complete field (not just one about memory) was due to similar achievements being made at roughly the same time by many other researchers and scientists addressing other aspects of cognition, including linguists and computer scientists.

It is commonly accepted that World War II also encouraged the growth of the discipline in at least two ways. First, research usually requires money to make it happen. Military interest in a variety of topics such as vigilance, creativity, attention and perception meant that cognitive psychologists were able to obtain military funding to advance their research. Furthermore, the more unfortunate consequence of war was that casualties suffering from brain injuries offered opportunities to study the relationship between the mind and the brain in ways that were not possible before.

The development of cognitive psychology as an area of study was also helped by the publication of the book *Cognitive Psychology* (Neisser, 1967, which solidified not only the name but the topic of study, and the importance of information-processing models for it. This was followed by journals dedicated to publishing original research in this field such as *Cognitive Psychology, Cognition* and *Memory & Cognition*, as well as national and international conferences, dedicated research laboratories, and research teams across the world. It was an exciting time for cognitive psychology and an important point in the discipline's history.

Cognition and behaviourism

In telling the story of the origins of cognitive psychology, attention is often given to the differences between the types of theories cognitive psychologists wanted to develop and the types of theories that other psychologists, particularly behaviourists, wanted to develop. **Behaviourism**, in very simple terms, is the idea that psychology can be studied by looking at relationships between behaviours without needing to theorise about things such as a mind. Now, like the definition of cognitive psychology, there would be some debate about this exact definition. For our purposes, this 'strong' form of behaviourism is interesting because it highlights an important aspect of cognitive psychology. Where behaviourists avoid theories about the internal structures of our minds, cognitive psychologists rely upon them when presenting their ideas and theories. This challenges us (and people past) to question what the best approach is: one in which we look at behaviours only; or one in which we believe we can make claims about internal mental processes and the structure of the mind. In terms of popularity, cognitive psychologists 'won'. They have been a meaningful part of mainstream psychology for the past 50 years.

Task — In your own words, describe the difference between cognitive psychology and the strong form of behaviourism as presented here. Which of the two versions do you consider to be the best? Why?

Cognitive psychology today

Cognitive psychology remains an integral part of modern psychology. The number of journals that publish original research continues to grow as researchers begin to turn their attention to how cognitive psychology can inform other disciplines. Teachers and researchers of cognitive psychology continue to be supported by dedicated research laboratories, national and international societies, and national and international conferences as well as constantly advancing technologies and the development of new and interesting methods. Students of psychology across the world are exposed to the ideas, theories and methods of cognitive psychology as central parts of their curriculum, with many of them becoming the new generation of researchers and teachers in many different countries. To cut a long story short, cognitive psychology is a healthy (and happy) part of modern-day psychology.

The nature of science

You have learned that an important part of cognitive psychology is that it is the scientific study of the mind. This emphasis on science is not limited to cognitive psychology – it is a feature of lots of psychology in general. However, it is part of our definition of cognitive psychology so it is important that we understand what it means for the types of ideas that are generated, theories that are formed, and research that is conducted.

Critical thinking activity

Scientifically proven?

Critical thinking focus: reflection

Key question: *What are your assumptions about what makes science?*

As you have learned, a strict adherence to the scientific method is very important for cognitive psychology. In this activity you will practise a skill known as reflection. Broadly speaking, reflection is when you think in depth about your experiences, action, feelings and responses to them in a way that you might usually not think about.

In this activity we want you to reflect upon when you have seen a product advertised with the claim that it is 'scientifically proven'. This may be a face cream or cosmetic product, or it could be an indigestion remedy or a probiotic yoghurt. Think back on this experience and answer the following questions.

What did you think at the time?

How did you feel about the product?

Did you believe it would achieve whatever it claimed to? If yes, why? If no, why not?

Continue to reflect about the experience beyond these few questions. Ask yourself how you felt (suspicious? excited?), what you did (bought it? laughed at it?), and how you generally reacted (dismissive? believing?). Think deeply about these reflections and try to understand what these mean for you and how you think about science. Try to answer the question: what criteria do you personally have for something to be scientific?

Critical thinking review

This activity helps develop your reflection skills while thinking about the nature of science. In particular, this activity gives you an opportunity to step back and notice things you may not have done previously. For example, you may discover beliefs you never realised you had or behaviours that you were not consciously aware that you were doing. You may notice that your feelings may affect how you think about things. Being able to take a step back and look at experiences from a distance helps you identify these assumptions or biases you may have, and how they may be clouding your thinking.

> Being able to reflect on experiences in this way is an important skill to develop as you move away from being a passive observer of the world to someone who thinks critically about it. In the 'real world' such skills are crucial in making sense of one's own experiences, and reactions to them, such as in the work place.
>
> Other skills you may have used in this activity include: analysing and evaluating, and comparison.

As with other definitions, there is some debate as to what science is. There are a number of key features of science that will help us distinguish it from other sources of information such as experience or pseudoscience. These are (in no particular order):

- **falsifiability**;

- **objectivity**;

- **replicability**.

You will learn about each of these features in turn.

Falsifiability

The term falsifiability comes from 'falsify' and is the claim that for an idea or theory to be scientific it must be possible to test whether it is false. If there is no way to test that it is false (i.e. not true), then that theory or idea cannot be seen as scientific. This is particularly true of statements or theories that include ideas such as supernatural forces or that appeal to the ideas of mystery or other-worldly control. If there is no way to show these claims are false, then we cannot consider these ideas to be scientific.

Objectivity

Objectivity is the idea that measurements of psychological phenomena should not be influenced by personal interpretation. For example, if someone claims to be able to remember things very well, but they can only do it in their head and by the time they come to say it they have forgotten it, then their amazing memory feat is not objective because no one else can ever observe it (it is the opposite, it is subjective). Because we cannot directly observe something like memory or attention, cognitive psychologists use something known as an **operational definition**. The purpose of this operational definition is to define the aspect of the mind in a way that can be observed and measured by other people. For example, the operational definition of memory may be performance on a particular memory test, or an average score on a number of different tests.

As theories change, so will the operational definitions that different researchers use, often referring to finer definitions of the topic of study (for example, short-term memory or divided attention). Whatever the operational definition of the aspect of the mind, it is important that it is clear and is something that someone else could observe. Whether the operational definition is appropriate is often an important point of analysis and evaluation.

Replicability

Closely related to falsifiability and objectivity is the idea of replicability: that other researchers can replicate the main findings of the research. It is all very well studying something that others can observe, but if they do not observe the same thing, then the claim must be challenged or modified to explain this. This is very important because every good cognitive psychologist must be able to accept this idea. No matter how much you believe in a theory, or personal experience, if no one else finds the same thing, then it must be questioned. If the idea isn't questioned, then it isn't being treated in a scientific way.

These are just a few features of what makes science, and you may be able to think of more. What is important is that you are able to distinguish science from other types of claims based on experience or **pseudoscience**.

Experience and pseudoscience

Whereas scientific claims can be falsifiable, observable and replicable, claims based on experience and pseudoscience do not follow these rules. For example, a claim of having seen a ghost is based upon experience but is impossible to falsify: no one else can observe it (if it happened in the past), and it is most likely that no one else can replicate this finding. This is therefore a claim made upon experience only, and cannot be thought of as a scientific claim. Now that example was chosen because it was fairly clear cut. Another example might be an individual claiming that a particular problem, say a memory problem, was solved by visiting someone who claims to be a healer. Again, to verify the memory-restoring properties of the healer in a scientific way it would have to be possible to observe it, replicate it, and find a way to falsify it.

Consider now that the same person is claiming that they improved their memory through completing a crossword puzzle every day for a year. Now we may be able to falsify this one by getting many different participants, and having them do the same thing. We would have to consider an operational definition of memory (if based on more than their memory 'feeling' better) and we would have to find an improvement just as they claimed (replication). Now consider the same person claiming they have been chewing some herb in their garden and it has improved their memory. Again, to consider this a scientific claim, the same standards apply.

We have thought about this range of examples because you may find some more believable than others. It is tempting (and often happens) that we are happier to consider something as a scientific claim if we personally believe it is true. However, it is important that we get out of thinking this way and evaluate all of these claims with the same criteria. If it fails to meet one of the criteria, then it is not scientific.

Methods of cognitive psychology

You have learned that scientific method is important for the identity of cognitive psychology. Part of this scientific method is to make direct observations of what we are interested in and to measure them. If you think about it, this creates a specific problem for cognitive psychology because we are interested in things that are not directly observable: mental processes. To get around this we have to observe and measure human behaviour, and then draw conclusions from these observations about mental processes or structures. This mostly involves using carefully designed experiments in which something that we are interested in is systematically altered (the **independent variable**) and what happens to our measure (**dependent variable**) is directly observed. The range of things that have been systematically varied across the decades will become apparent as you read through this book and learn about the many varied questions cognitive psychologists have tried to answer. The following sections briefly cover two types of measurements that can be taken.

Reaction times

One common measure is to see how fast or slow people are at doing certain behaviours, or completing certain tasks. This measurement is known as a **reaction time**. The logic goes that if someone is faster (or slower) at completing a specific task when you change something, then what you changed influences the mental processes that are involved (or at least the speed of them). We can illustrate this with an example.

Logan and Crump (2009) were interested in whether paying attention to a skill (in this case typing) reduced the ability to do it. This research began with the simple observation that if you are skilled at doing something, paying attention to what you are doing can make you worse at it. In their study they recruited some touch typists. These are skilled typists who have learned a set of rules about which letters each hand types. A touch typist will use their left hand to type certain letters and their right hand to type the other letters. The typists they used were highly proficient. On average they typed over 60 words per minute on a typing test (that's more than one word every second). Logan and Crump (2009) tested a very specific theory that they had developed about why paying attention to a skill might make it worse. The details of this theory are not important here; what *is* important is that they made some very specific predictions based on this theory. One of these predictions was that any disruptive influence of attention applies only when people focus attention on what they are doing (the output) but not when attention is focused on what they are doing it to (the input). In the example of the typists, focusing attention on what each hand is doing may be disruptive but focusing attention on what needs to be typed might not.

For example, across several experiments Logan and Crump (2009) had touch typists complete typing tests in different ways. Participants were shown four-letter words on a computer screen and were required to type them. Before each word, they were instructed how to type them. Sometimes they were asked to type the whole word as they saw it; sometimes they were asked to type only the letters associated with the left hand, and other times they were asked to type only the letters associated with the right hand. The idea behind this manipulation was that paying attention to which hand types which letters would make the touch typists slightly worse at the task. The main measurement that was taken was how fast they produced a correct response. You have learned already that this measure is also known as a reaction time. The results of this experiment were that touch typists were slower to type words when they had to pay attention to the correspondence between their hands and the letters associated with each. This suggests that focusing attention on what you are doing may reduce your ability to execute a skill. You may be able to think of some other explanations here. Before you dwell too long on those, let's look at another very similar experiment from the same study.

In another experiment in this study the participants completed an almost identical task to that described above. The difference was that instead of being asked to type the whole word, letters associated with the left hand, or letters associated with the right hand, participants were instead asked to type the whole word, or letters coloured in green, or letters coloured in red. The words presented to them were either all in black type, or they had the letters related to the left hand coloured in red, or they had the letters related to the right hand coloured in green. The same physical responses were therefore required in this experiment as in the experiment described above. The main difference between the two was that participants in the first experiment were paying attention to the hands they usually use to type certain letters, but in this experiment they were paying attention to the colour of the letters. Importantly, these participants were not the same as those who took part in the experiment described above so there was no chance that they were practised at this task. Once again, the measurement used in this task was the reaction time of the participants (how long they took to type the words). The results of this second experiment were striking. There was no evidence of any disruption when the typists focused their attention on the colours of the letters, even though the same physical responses were required as the first experiment.

Across the two experiments it was found that the typists were slower to type letters in words when their attention was focused on typing specific letters that corresponded with certain hands, but typists were not slower to type letters in words when their attention was focused on the colour of the specific letters. This reduction in reaction time in one set of circumstances, but not in the other, supports the hypothesis that skilled behaviour is disrupted by attention focused on the output (in this case the correspondence between hands and letters) but not when attention is focused on the input (in this case typing letters in a certain colour). In turn, this supports the theoretical explanation that Logan and Crump (2009) had developed about skilled behaviour. We will not go into any further details about this here.

This example is important because it illustrates a number of principles that you have already learned in this chapter. The researchers were interested in the mental processes involved in skilled behaviour, particularly processes of attention. Because attention is not something we can look directly at (it is in our minds), they devised a careful series of experiments to tell them something about the mental processes. These experiments included something they could observe and measure, reaction time. In order to understand the influence of attention, they systematically altered where they asked participants to allocate their attention (to hands or to colours) while keeping the task exactly the same. Differences in what they observed (the time in which the tasks were completed) led them to believe that their hypothesis was supported. From this they argued that their more general theory about how the mind works with skilled behaviour was (for the time being) supported. And so a simple measure such as reaction time was used as a means to develop a more **abstract** theory about one way in which the mind works. That they used the scientific method to study the processes of the mind makes this cognitive psychology.

Task — Using the example above, try to think of another measurement the researchers could have taken. Think about what you do when you type and what could be measured. Is it possible to measure more than just how fast you type? Also think about what predictions you might make. Here the researchers argue that disruption of mental processes is reflected in slower reaction times. What would be the argument for your alternative measurement(s)?

Accuracy

An alternative to measuring how fast someone does something is to measure how accurately they do something. Again, the logic is that if someone is more accurate (or less accurate) at completing a specific task when something is systematically altered, then what was altered influences the mental processes that are involved. Again, you might find it easier to think about this using an example (this one is briefer than the last).

Wilford and Wells (2010) were interested in how people mentally process changes in faces compared to other things. They started with the observation that when people make changes to their facial appearance, close acquaintances and family tend to notice that something has changed but can't always say what. Their starting point in the existing literature was the general finding that people process faces in ways that are different from how they process other objects (such as cars, houses or objects in a room). More specifically, it is believed that people tend to process faces as a 'whole' more than they do with objects. Wilford and Wells (2010) argued that processing a face as a 'whole' might help people detect changes, but it might make them less able to say *what* has changed. For them, this hypothesis explained their initial observation, but they needed to gather some evidence to support it.

In their experiment their main manipulation was to show people pictures of either faces or houses (the independent variable). They then showed them another picture that might, or might not, have changed. One measure of accuracy they took was whether people could correctly say if there had been a change. Taking this measure, it was generally found that people were more accurate at detecting changes in pictures of faces than pictures of houses. This suggests that when we are detecting a change in a face the mental processes are different compared to detecting changes in other objects.

In this experiment, Wilford and Wells (2010) also showed people pictures of faces or pictures of houses, then showed them a picture that the participants were told had definitely changed. The measure of accuracy they then took was to see if people could identify *what* had changed (from a choice of five possibilities). When this measure was taken, it was generally found that people were more accurate at identifying what had changed with pictures of *houses* rather than faces. What was found from these measurements of accuracy therefore supported the idea that when people know there is a change, they are better at saying where that change is with houses than with faces.

Once again it is useful to highlight how this example of accuracy being used as a measure in cognitive psychology illustrates the principles that you have learned. The researchers were interested in the mental processes involved in perceiving faces, particularly the way in which the information is processed. Because the mental processing of faces is not something we can look at directly (it is in our minds), they devised a careful experiment to answer questions about these processes. This experiment included something they could observe and measure, the accuracy of participant responses. In order to understand the difference between the mental processing of faces and the processing of other objects, they systematically altered the pictures they asked participants to make judgements about (pictures of faces or pictures of houses). They also systematically altered the type of task that participants had to complete (saying if a change had occurred, saying what change had occurred). Differences in what they observed (the accuracy of the judgements) led them to believe that their hypothesis was supported. From this they argued that their more general theory about how faces are processed could be developed to include their findings. And so a simple measure such as accuracy was used as a means to develop a more abstract theory about one way in which the mind works. That they used the scientific method to study the processes of the mind again makes this cognitive psychology.

Skill builder activity

Measuring the mind

Transferable skill focus: information technology

Key question: *What measurements are cognitive psychologists currently using?*

You have learned about two measurements that cognitive psychologists might take in order to investigate the workings of the mind: reaction times and accuracy. However, these aren't the only measures that people can take. With this activity we will make use of the internet to explore what other measures cognitive psychologists use.

On a computer open up an internet browser (such as Internet Explorer, Firefox or Google Chrome) and navigate to a suitable search tool (such as www.google.co.uk or www.bing.co.uk). Then search for the homepage of a journal that publishes articles about cognitive psychology – you learned about three of them earlier. The easiest to search for would be the journal *Cognitive Psychology*: use the search terms 'cognitive psychology journal'.

Click on the link to the journal homepage when you have found it. On these homepages you will find a short description of the journal as well as links to articles that have been recently published. If they are not on the homepage, there will be links to an appropriate table of contents or lists of issues where you will be able to find examples of articles they publish. Choose an article that has a title that interests you. Use the links on the site to view the **abstract**. The abstract is a short summary of the article and is all you need for this activity. Read the abstract and try to determine what type of measurement they took. What the researchers did is usually found in the middle of the abstract, so look there. It is also important that you read the first half of the abstract (to see what they did and why) and the last half of the abstract (to see what they found and what they think it means).

Repeat this exercise for three or four more abstracts (you may find you have to skip some where you cannot work out what the measure is). See how many of these measured reaction times or accuracy, and see how many used a different measure.

Skill builder review

This activity helps develop your information technology skills, by focusing on your ability to search for and navigate around the homepages of journals. These homepages provide lots of useful information and links to original research articles in the field of cognitive psychology. This is most useful when you are generally browsing what is new in the field of cognitive psychology. When you have a very specific question in mind there are more efficient ways to search for articles using search tools that look at specific databases (rather than the whole web). PsycINFO and PubMED are two examples of these databases, and they are discussed in more detail in the skill builder in Chapter 3 (Learning and memory).

Other skills you may have used in this activity include: analysis and evaluation; comparison; and decision making.

Cognitive psychology in your life

Sometimes the ideas and theories of cognitive psychology may seem so unlike what happens in your life that their relevance will be unclear. One thing we will do together in this book is to think about how the ideas and theories we discuss are related to things that you see, you do and you think about every day. One important idea that is important for all of this is the idea that cognition is so much a part of our everyday lives that we often take it for granted until something goes wrong.

Imagine, if you can, what it would be like to have no memory – that is, for every person you meet, it feels like you are meeting them for the first time and you have no idea who they are or why they might want to talk to you. Imagine that you only ever pay attention to the left side of space, with the events in the right side of space a complete mystery to you even though you can see them perfectly well. Imagine that you aren't able to recognise an object if someone turned it to a slightly different angle, or are unable to see if something is moving or still. Imagine that you can only ever find one solution to any problem, or that the letters of words move around as you try to read them. That most of us don't have these experiences like these is often taken for granted.

Predominantly, cognitive psychologists are keen to understand what happens in the 'normal' mind. How we decide what is a normal mind (versus an abnormal mind) is itself a major challenge and not one we are going to discuss here. It is worth noting that cognitive psychologists tend to ignore individual differences between people (apart from perhaps a normal/abnormal distinction) and work on the basis that we can try to **generalise** from one normal mind (or a sample of them) to other normal minds. This isn't perfect, and these assumptions can be challenged (and have been frequently). You will learn later on that analysis and evaluation isn't just about highlighting problems about an approach but also about understanding what can be learned from it. The enduring nature of cognitive psychology reflects the idea that there is still a lot to be gained from it. If someone were to come up with an alternative that helped to answer questions about the mind scientifically while resolving these criticisms (and not introducing new weakness) then I am certain many cognitive psychologists would embrace it.

Task — Think of one thing you have done today (it really can be anything). Try to list things about it that may involve those aspects of cognitive psychology that have been mentioned. For example, did you need to remember anything to do it? Was this conscious or unconscious? Did you have to perceive anything to do this (particular shapes or depth)? Did you have to make any decisions, or solve any problems? Did it involve understanding a language at all (such as English), either written or spoken? Did you have to focus your attention on it, or could you be distracted? All of these topics (and more) form cognitive psychology.

Assignments

1. Defend the idea that cognitive psychology must use the scientific method. Outline what you believe to be some of the advantages and some of the disadvantages of using the scientific method. Present these so that you can defend the idea that the scientific method is important.

2. Describe how the topic areas of cognitive psychology apply in everyday life. Use two examples of behaviour you do on a daily basis to illustrate your points.

3. Compare and contrast scientific and non-scientific explanations for behaviours. Construct an example that you could explain in a scientific way and in a non-scientific way, outlining the main ways in which the two differ. Argue the benefits of having a scientific explanation in reference to this example.

Summary: what you have learned

You have learned that cognitive psychology has a relatively short history but has taken a prominent place in mainstream psychology. In taking this place, cognitive psychology was contrasted with the behaviourist perspective that was less willing to theorise about mental structures and processes.

You also now know how important the scientific method is to cognitive psychology, and you have learned about concepts such as falsifiability, objectivity and replicability. With these terms you have begun to understand the difference between science and pseudoscience (or experience).

Finally, the importance of cognition in everyday life has been highlighted, and you now understand just how important cognition is to our everyday experiences (and why it is such an interesting area of study).

You have also had the opportunity to develop your information technology skills in terms of accessing summaries of up-to-date cognitive research, and you have had the chance to develop your reflective skills when considering the assumptions that you have about science.

Further reading

Bermudez, JL (2010) *Cognitive science: an introduction to the science of the mind*. Cambridge: Cambridge University Press.

An excellent accessible book that looks at the broader field of cognitive science, demonstrating how the findings of cognitive psychology and other fields can be integrated for a better understanding of the mind.

Eysenck, MW and Keane, MT (2010) *Cognitive psychology: a student's handbook*. 6th edition. London: Psychology Press.

This textbook provides a comprehensive and more detailed overview of cognitive psychology. Ideal for more advanced reading on the basic topics presented here.

Wilshire, C (2012) *Cognitive neuropsychology: exploring the mind through brain dysfunction*. London: Psychology Press.

A useful introduction to cognitive neuropsychology, this provides more comprehensive coverage of the relationship between possible mental structures of the mind and the physical brain.

Chapter 2

Thinking and reasoning

Learning outcomes

By the end of this chapter you should:

- *be able to evaluate different perspectives on how we categorise concepts;*

- *be able to discuss theoretical approaches to how we solve problems;*

- *be able to analyse bias and heuristics in decision making;*

- *be able to complete an analysis and evaluation of different theoretical approaches, and have developed your problem-solving skills.*

Introduction

Do you know what I'm thinking? This is a question you will be asked a lot if you tell people you like psychology. Unfortunately, nothing in this chapter will help you answer that question in a polite way. Nevertheless, this chapter *will* open your eyes to what is an intriguing area for many psychologists: thinking and reasoning. We have already defined cognitive psychology as the scientific study of the mind as an information processor. As thinking is a mental process we use all the time, the study of thinking becomes an important topic in cognitive psychology. This chapter focuses on three significant areas of research:

- how we categorise and conceptualise things;

- how we solve problems;

- how we make decisions.

It will guide you through thinking critically about the theories and research in each of these subjects, as well as examining the many interesting findings that dominate this compelling area.

The importance of concepts and categories

Why, out of all the topics in the world, would we want to start here? The human ability to categorise and conceptualise is part of the foundations for our perception, learning, memory and language (to name but a few). But what are concepts and categories? And what is the difference between the two?

A concept is generally defined as a mental representation of classes of objects or other entities. In other words, a concept is a general idea that you can apply to examples of things. To illustrate: think about the concept 'chair'. The chances are you are sitting on something that might belong to your concept of what a 'chair' is. It is also likely that this idea you have does not only apply to the 'chair' you are sitting on. If you think for a little bit, you will be able to come up with other examples of 'chairs' that you have seen in your life. You therefore have a mental representation of chairs (the concept) that covers a certain class of objects (what you call chairs). This last idea is important. In formal terms a category is a class of objects embodied in concepts. To put this in simple terms, concepts are in our heads (mental representations) while a category is something in the real world that exists. You can reach out and touch a member of a category, but you can't touch the concept. This applies to things that exist in the real world (**concrete** categories). We will come back to things that don't exist in quite the same physical way (abstract categories) later on.

You were probably happy enough with the chair example. If you ask other members of your family or friends, you may all roughly agree what the concept of a chair is. Why would psychologists be interested in this? If you stop and think about it, the world could be divided up in almost limitless ways. The word 'could' is important because, although the possibilities are endless, there are only a small number of ways that have any meaning to us. So how do humans decide upon what is in a category or isn't in a category? And what is or isn't included in a concept? What started out as something quite simple is actually quite complicated.

To try to unravel at least some of this puzzle we will look at three approaches to capturing how we conceptualise and categorise things:

- classical (defining-attribute) approach;
- prototype approach;
- exemplar approach.

We will look at each of these in turn.

Classical approach

More often than not you will find lectures (and textbooks) starting with lots of detail about the history of an idea. It is reasonable to question if it is worth it: why don't we just start with the latest ideas? The reasoning is simple: how we view things is more often than not coloured by the past. As theories or approaches develop, they must account for not only the very latest evidence or information but also everything that went before it. To understand where we are now, we need to know where we have been. Importantly, it clearly demonstrates the kind of critical thinking that has occurred through the development of the ideas. We start here with an idea that was first articulated (in recorded form) by the Greek philosopher Aristotle (Sutcliffe, 1993).

Aristotle suggested that any concept is understood by its defining features. That is, for any concept there exists a list of features that makes something a member of it. These lists consist of a number of features that something must have in order to be part of a concept. If something has all those features, then it is in. If it doesn't have all of those features, then it is out. This means that everything that is part of a concept has an equal status. Each member of that concept is equally representative of it.

Task — Choose an object in your current location and make a list of all its features that you can think of. Then think of another example of this object elsewhere and make a list of all the features of that too. Compare the two. Are you able to come up with a list of defining features that includes both examples equally?

Aristotle clearly didn't mean there was a physical set of lists somewhere (perhaps hidden in a cave or under the sea), but he did mean that there were mental lists, or agreed sets of attributes, that define a concept. That is, a concept is a psychological phenomenon that sets us a nice challenge. With enough hard work, study and data gathering, we should, in theory, be able to find all of these defining attributes for any given concept or category. On the surface, this may seem intuitively appealing, and fairly straightforward. The alternative view is that concepts are more fuzzy than this (see Zadeh, 1965). So let's do some mental gymnastics and try to think this one through.

Here is a simple question for you: Is a banana a herb? That is, does a banana belong to your concept of a herb? It may surprise you to learn that it is a herb, but that may not mean you consider it to be. Here are a few more questions taken from an influential study by McCloskey and Glucksberg (1978):

- Is a poet an animal?

- Is a penguin a bird?

- Is advertising a science?

In their study, McCloskey and Glucksberg (1978) asked 30 college students to rate 540 pairs such as those above. The students' task was to decide whether each example (e.g. poet, penguin, advertising) is a member of a category (e.g. animal, bird, science). What emerged from studies such as this is that people are inconsistent in what they consider to be a member of a category. This inconsistency is between people (different people give different responses) and within people (if asked to do this sort of thing twice, people change their minds, giving different responses the second time around).

Think now about a more abstract concept that is currently very popular: the X Factor. Try to write down a list of 'features' that define someone who has the X Factor. Remember, to support the classical approach – everyone who has the X Factor must have everything you put on this list, and everyone who belongs to this concept must be equally representative of the X Factor. This is not an easy task. Some people have it; some people don't. Some people have it and lose it; some people never have it; and some people never had it but somehow got it at a later point. Importantly, it is difficult to define but there is nevertheless agreement that it exists, even if there is some disagreement about who or what falls under it. It therefore exists as a concept but in a 'fuzzy' way. This is problematic for any theory that suggests all members of a category are equal. There is evidence to suggest that the idea of 'typicality' can help resolve this to some extent.

Typicality

When answering the question 'Is a penguin a bird?' you may have said: 'A penguin is a bit birdy – I don't know'; 'A penguin is technically a bird, but it isn't very bird like'; or 'Given the research findings of Rips et al. (1973), I reject the classical approach to understanding concepts that clearly underpins the question that has been posed to me and instead insist on rating the penguin according to its typicality within this category, in which case the notion that a penguin is a bird is clarified with the statement that I do not consider it to be a typical bird'. Maybe you wouldn't give the last answer, but it is an important point. Any concept or category clearly has members that are more typical than others. Every member is not equally representative. We can do fairly well if asked to rate how 'typical' something is (although we can sometimes struggle, but we'll deal with that later). This has knock-on effects for our cognitive processes. For example, we are able to decide whether something is typical of a category more quickly than whether it is atypical (Rips, Shoben and Smith, 1973), and we are able to learn new concepts quicker if given examples of typical members rather than atypical members (Mervis and Pani, 1980). That is, 'typicality' influences how we think about things (at least in terms of speed of learning and decision making).

Task ── In your own words, describe why typicality is a useful idea when thinking about concepts and categories.

Let's stop for a moment and consider the classical defining-attribute approach. In many ways it has lots to offer. It is precise and interpretable (people understand what it says and can grasp the details). It is very testable (it is worded in such a way that it is possible to find evidence against it). Unfortunately, it doesn't describe the evidence we have collected (and the evidence presented here is a very small part of what exists). Is there an approach that can better account for the evidence that we do have?

Prototype approach

An alternative to the classical approach is the prototype approach (Rosch and Mervis, 1975). This approach suggests that there is a central description (prototype) that somehow represents the category or concept. This prototype is regarded by some as a list of characteristics in which some are given more importance (weight) than others. Compared to the classical view, this approach suggests there are no defining attributes, just characteristic ones. Common features across members of a category are known as 'family resemblances'.

This may sound a bit like the classical approach because it relies upon similarity. One important difference between the two approaches is that the classical approach requires all of the defining attributes to exist if something is to be 'in'. In comparison, the prototype approach is not so strict and allows things 'in' even if they don't match exactly. Hence, a penguin falls under the concept of a bird but is not a typical bird.

As with the classical approach, there is some evidence that cannot be accounted for by a strong version of the prototype approach (as presented here). For example, circumstances (**context**) play an important part in any beliefs about category membership (Barsalou, 1987, 1989). To illustrate this, asking visitors to a bird sanctuary if a penguin is a bird may produce different responses to asking visitors to a zoo the same question. Attributes that help define different concepts may be very unstable and dependent on the context, and this is known as **context-dependent** information (Barsalou, 1982).

Task ⎯ Think of another example where context may change the category people say something was in. What category would they say it belonged to in the first set of circumstances? And in another set of circumstances?

The examples here have mainly included 'chairs' and 'penguins'. These concepts refer to concrete concepts because chairs and penguins do physically exist. Let's think about concepts that are not represented in the physical world (abstract concepts). While you could easily point to a chair or find an example of a typical chair, could you show someone a belief or point out a typical instinct? It is much more difficult, some may say impossible (e.g. Hampton, 1981), to specify prototypes for abstract concepts. Any concept may also depend on the experiences you have had in your life (Malt and Smith, 1982). If your parents always referred to a flower pot as a chair, would it be part of your concept of chairs? The exemplar approach to categorisation may help us here.

Exemplar approach

The exemplar approach (Kruschke, 1992; Nosofsky, 1986, 1991) provides one of the most substantial challenges to the prototype approach. Rather than consider concepts as mental representations, based upon feature lists, the exemplar approach assumes that concepts are formed from specific instances in your past experiences. Past experiences are stored in human memory, and these instances are used when judging if something is part of a concept.

Exemplar approaches can account for many of the same research findings as the prototype approach. For example, when judging whether a robin is a typical bird, people are often quicker to make the judgement than when judging if a robin is an animal (Rips, Shoben and Smith, 1973). The prototype approach suggests that a robin may be more 'like' a prototype of a bird than it is 'like' a prototype of an animal. In contrast, the exemplar approach suggests that people are quicker to classify a robin as a bird because it is more like the examples that come to mind when thinking about birds than when thinking about animals.

An important difference between the exemplar approach and the prototype approach is the extent to which they consider 'general rules' or 'regularities' to be important. For the prototype approach this abstraction of general rules (a prototype) is very important, while for the exemplar approach everything is based upon sets of specific instances with no abstract summary. Evidence suggests that while the exemplar approach can account for complex concepts, it cannot do as well with simple concepts (Smith and Minda, 2000), and it is likely that these different approaches may work best for different circumstances (or sets of evidence).

Task — In your own words, summarise the main difference between the exemplar approach and the prototype approach. Use an example to illustrate the points you make.

We have presented these approaches as two distinct alternatives – that either one or the other must happen. However, recent developments suggest that people may actually use a compromise between these two extremes when making the sorts of judgements found in research (Van Paemel and Storms, 2008).

Critical thinking activity

Fuzzy concepts

Critical thinking focus: analysing and evaluating

Key question: Which is the best approach to understanding how we use categories and concepts in everyday life: the classical approach, the prototype approach or the exemplar approach?

Critical thinking isn't just about being negative or 'putting down' what passes for knowledge, but instead uses reasoning, problem solving, and decision-making skills to analyse and evaluate what we know, and what further questions we have to answer.

To help you to do this, draw a large table with the following details. In the far left column put the heading 'theoretical approach', and underneath this insert three rows labelled classical approach, prototype approach and exemplar approach. Use the columns of the table to make notes about these approaches against a number of criteria. The following criteria need one column each.

Evidence. (Does the approach describe the evidence we have available? To what extent? Give examples.)

Precision. (Are the ideas precise? Is there anything ambiguous in the theory? Give examples.)

Interpretation. (Is it clear how the approach can be used to interpret evidence? Give examples.)

Overall. (Give an overall analysis of the approach based on your answers in the previous columns.)

Complete the table using the information you have here. Once you have completed the table, you should have not only an overall evaluation but also some reasoning as to why you have reached these conclusions. If you feel adventurous, read other textbooks or journal articles to see if you can fill out more information in each column. You may find that this changes your overall analysis.

Critical thinking review

This activity helps develop your analysis and evaluation skills in relation to how we define concepts and categorise things. You were encouraged to use a specific set of criteria (evidence, precision and interpretation). These criteria are only a few of those that people have used to analyse and evaluate theoretical approaches. You may also think about: whether the approach is as simple as it could be; if it is different from other theories; if it applies to a broad range of phenomena (or very specific ones); if it is possible to test the theories; and if the theory only describes what is already known.

Being able to analyse and evaluate information in this way is an important skill to develop as you move away from being a passive recipient of information to being an active and critical thinker who takes part in the development of knowledge. In the 'real world' such skills are crucial in making sense of the world in an informed and intelligent way.

Other skills you may have used in this activity include: reflection; critical thinking; decision making; independent learning; and problem solving.

Problem solving and how to improve it

Complete an application for a job, or go to a job interview, and you may well say that you are a good problem solver. Indeed, we fear for anyone in those situations who admits they are not very good at solving problems. It is beyond imagining that any candidate for a job would declare that they tend to use one type of solution and can't see around it (negative set) or that they are unable to think about novel ways of using things (functional fixedness). However, research suggests that these are two of the things that we actually do when faced with problems. This next section of the chapter looks at some of the other factors that have an influence when solving problems, and how to become better problem solvers.

Insight

As always, we will start with the roots of early approaches to problem solving: **Gestalt psychology**. The term **Gestalt** is associated with a group of German psychologists and researchers who published most of their work at the start of the twentieth century. *Gestalt* indicates a particular approach to human psychology that argues that we deal with things as 'wholes' rather than individual parts. It is argued that it is not useful to study the individual parts, as they tell us nothing about the whole. This may seem a bit abstract so we'll look at an example. Imagine you are listening to a song and you wanted to know the melody. It would not be enough to find out every single note on its own. Put them together in different orders and you can produce many different melodies. That is, the whole melody is different from each of the individual notes added together. If we want to understand the melody, we need to study it as a whole.

In more general terms, *Gestalt* psychology is heavily associated with the phrase *the whole is different from the sum of its parts*. But what does this have to do with problem solving?

In the 1920s, a famous *Gestalt* psychologist named Wolfgang Köhler was interested in problem solving in apes (not humans). Most famously, Köhler (1925) had an ape participant known as 'Sultan'. One problem Sultan had to solve was the following: he was stuck in a cage, while some bananas (presumably his favourite food) were outside the cage and he was not able to reach them through the bars. At first Sultan used a long stick to move the bananas towards the cage until he was able to grab them. This represented a basic level of problem solving in which another object (the stick) was used to solve the problem. To make the problem harder for Sultan, Köhler removed the long stick from his cage and replaced it with two shorter sticks. The story goes that Sultan was initially unable to solve the problem; the change of sticks meant his original solution no longer worked. After a while Sultan joined the two shorter sticks together. Having joined them together he was once more able to move the bananas to his cage and reach out for them. It was concluded by Köhler, alongside other evidence, that apes were capable of the 'ah-ha' moment in problem solving that we refer to as insight learning. This was important because it challenged the existing notion that problems were only solved by 'learning' solutions through trial and error. The most important contribution of Köhler was to challenge this notion, suggesting that problems can also be solved through sudden insights. These claims stimulated lots of research, this time with human subjects.

Task — In your own words, describe the difference between solving problems by trial and error and solving problems using insight. Try to generate new examples from your own experience to illustrate your thoughts.

Human insight and analogy

So what is meant by human insight? Insight is often talked about as an 'ah-ha' moment: that is, a moment in which a novel approach to a problem, or a new way of looking upon things, is suddenly realised.

Sometimes good problem solving comes from an insight that uses an **analogy**. This involves reasoning that if two things are alike in one respect, they may be similar in others. In our case, if two problems are similar in some way, then they may have similar solutions. You could have thought that this 'insight' thing sounds a lot like a 'Eureka' moment – this common phrase actually has its roots in insight learning by analogy.

The story goes that the Greek scientist Archimedes was asked to work out if the king's crown was made from solid gold, or if silver had been mixed into it as well. Archimedes was able to work out the weights of both gold and silver in terms of volume, but could not figure out how to calculate the volume of the crown. It is told that some time later, as Archimedes stepped into a bath, he noticed that the water rose as he got in. It was at this point that he realised the solution to his problem, and leapt out of the bath, ran naked through the streets, and yelled *Eureka!* (meaning *I have found it*). He had realised that he could use the amount of water displaced by the crown to work out the volume of the crown and therefore find out if it was pure gold. While there is no doubt this story may have changed in its telling, it provides a very useful example. Sudden insight can occur through finding the links between what you know about already and the problem you are trying to solve.

Task — Think of an example from your life of a problem that has been solved using an analogy. It may be an example from your experience, the experiences of friends, or even your family. Evaluate if the solution was a good one.

While analogies may help with sudden insight, people often miss the links unless they are clearly highlighted. For example, Gick and Holyoak (1980) gave their participants two problems that used very different topic areas (radiation and an army parade) but had very similar solutions. It was thought that participants who had solved the first problem would find it easier to solve the second one (given how similar they were). Interestingly, only 49 per cent of people solving the first problem were able to solve the second. Making the two problems appear to be more similar on the surface increased this number to 76 per cent, and then up to 92 per cent when participants were given a strong hint about the analogy. In control conditions where no hint was given, only 20 per cent of people came up with the correct solution. While problem solving by analogy may be very helpful, it is clear that we do not always do it spontaneously (or at least in the environment of an experiment).

Insight and drawing on analogy may seem intuitively appealing, yet some people argue that good problem solving is much more systematic than this. They suggest that there are a small number of general rules (also called **heuristics**, or 'rules of thumb') that help people move from the start of a problem to the end.

Heuristics and means–end analysis

Much of the work on heuristics in problem solving originates from the work of two people: Newell and Simon (1972). In their research they asked people to solve simple problems that they had written, and to say out loud what they were thinking. They then took what people said and identified some general rules that they seemed to be using. This was put into a computer program known as the General Problem Solver. Some of the most basic principles of this program were that people solve problems in sequential steps and that they can remember only a small amount of information that is new (in short-term memory) but they will make use of relevant information from the past that they can remember more easily (long-term memory). To make the move from one step to the next, it was suggested that people use a number of different 'rules of thumb'.

The general principle of means–end analysis is that trying to reach a solution (or 'goal') involves regularly, and repeatedly, assessing the difference between where you are at (current state) and where you want to be (the goal state or sub-goal state). Then you do something (apply an operator) that reduces the difference between where you are and where you want to be. For example, this may be setting a new sub-goal, and trying to achieve that.

Task — Consider a means–end analysis of one instance of problem solving from your own life. For example, if you have revised for an exam, what was your starting state (perhaps two months before the exam)? What was the main goal? How did you reduce the difference between the two? Did you set or use sub-goals to achieve this?

Research into means–end analysis has traditionally used quite a small number of problems to find out more about how we solve them. One well-known example is the missionary–cannibal problem. This is sometimes also known as the hobbits and orcs problem. We'll consider it in those terms:

> Three hobbits and three orcs are on one side of a river and need to cross to the other side. The only means of crossing is a boat, and the boat can only hold two people at a time. Devise a set of moves that will transport all six people across the river, bearing in mind the following constraint: the number of orcs can never exceed the number of hobbits in any location, for the obvious reason. Remember that someone will have to row the boat back across each time.

Task — Try to solve the hobbits and orcs problem. Talk out loud the steps that you are taking. Think about what you did and whether you used a means–end analysis. A full solution can easily be found online using the keywords: Missionaries Cannibals Problem.

The smallest number of moves needed to solve this problem is eleven, and many people make more moves than this and can even get stuck. The most interesting things for cognitive psychologists are the steps that people find most difficult. Those steps tell us something about how people solve problems. One of the most difficult steps in this problem, that many people struggle with, is to send two people back on the boat to the original side of the river (Thomas, 1974). Intuitively, we struggle with this although technically it is the correct thing to do. This therefore demonstrates that humans do not always solve problems in the most logical way. Interestingly the computer program that Newell and Simon (1972) created didn't struggle with this at all. This analogy between human and computer has been very helpful (as well as provocative), with more advanced computer programs such as ACT-R (Anderson et al., 2004) being developed from a means–end approach to account not only for human problem solving but also skills such as expertise.

Good problem solving

You have learned about some of the approaches taken to understanding problem solving. This is a rich area of research and if you explore it a little more, you will find many more problems, theories and approaches that are all fascinating.

It would be wrong to finish this section without some indication of how you may improve your own problem solving. What follows are a few simple suggestions from the broad findings in the available research.

Task — For each of the suggestions below think about how it might work for you. Make a note of any potential limitations or difficulties you think you may have in using it in general life. What you find will demonstrate the great potential of psychological research, but also the natural limitations of how experimental research applies to 'real world' problems.

Know your stuff

Knowing lots of information about the relevant area is also known as having '**domain** knowledge'. Extensive domain knowledge is generally associated with better problem solving. An expert's knowledge of an area is likely to be organised in such a way that it allows them to develop more effective solutions to problems. Much of the research that supports this idea comes from looking at the expertise of chess players (e.g. Chase and Simon, 1973), and it would be a good idea to question how much the benefits of expertise would apply in different domains of knowledge (**generalisability**).

Some people have suggested that too much domain knowledge may actually be a problem, especially when it comes to creative solutions. This is because experts may get stuck in a certain way of thinking about their problems (Wiley, 1998). This is most evident in the world of work where big organisations often bring in consultants from outside their organisation to help them solve problems that the consultants have little knowledge about.

Follow a plan

Making and following a plan is generally regarded as a good idea when problem solving. No doubt your former teachers advised you – and now lecturers will advise you – to make a plan when writing an essay or other assignment. This will involve setting sub-goals to help you achieve your goal, as well as regularly checking to see where you are now and where you want to be, and thinking about what you need to do to get there. This description alone should indicate to you that this advice is grounded in good means–end analysis (Newell and Simon, 1972). Further research to support this has shown that in long problems with many different steps a plan is particularly important (e.g. Bransford and Stein, 1993). However, it is important that this plan is constantly revised. Don't be afraid to change a sub-goal or set a new one, as long as it helps you to move from your current state to your final goal.

Look for links

You have learned already that good problem solving can come from reasoning with analogies. Look for links between the problem you are trying to solve and similar problems and experiences. Don't limit yourself to looking for one type of similarity – research has shown that several different types of similarity can help you solve a problem with an analogy. Chen (2002) suggested that similarity may be found in the steps or actions that are taken (procedural similarity), in the structure of the problems (structural similarity), or even in ways that seem irrelevant to the problem (superficial similarity). Noticing these similarities is the first step; making use of them is the second. Importantly, finding and using these similarities take time and patience (Bowden, 1985) and won't necessarily be a 'quick fix'.

Change your perspective

It is clear that we all learn and work in different ways. Some of us prefer words, some of us prefer numbers, and some of us prefer pictures (to name but a few). Looking at any problem from a different perspective is generally known as changing the 'representation' (how the problem is represented in your head). So if you are stuck on a particularly hard problem, go back and change how you are mentally representing parts of the problem. For example, if the information in the problem is mainly numbers, will using some mental images help? Consider several different ways of representing a problem. Changing how you mentally represent a problem may hide something of importance, but it may also highlight aspects that you had not previously noticed. Even saying things out loud may help in the early stages of problem solving (Ahlum-Heath and DiVesta, 1986).

Decision making and bias

If you don't mind me asking, why did you buy the top that you are wearing? Why are you reading this here? And why are you doing it there? These are not rude questions – they just illustrate the point that we are constantly making decisions. From the clothes we wear and the books we read, to our holiday destinations and parliamentary elections, humans are constantly required to make decisions. We don't always make the most rational or most logical decisions, and our lives are littered with wrong decisions that felt right at the time (as well as right decisions that felt wrong at the time). How are we making these decisions?

In very broad terms, theories of decision making fall into two camps:

- normative theories;

- descriptive theories.

Normative theories focus on how decisions *should* be made if we were all rational decision-making machines. Descriptive theories focus on how we actually make decisions. This section briefly outlines the normative theories and descriptive theories of decision making alongside the types of rules of thumb (heuristics) and biases we may rely on.

Normative theories

Early work in decision making was not initiated by psychologists but by economists. Lots of the original ideas are phrased in terms of risks and gambling: every decision you make is a gamble with certain risks attached, and decisions can be made by working out the 'value' of each particular outcome. This value is also known as 'utility' and is a key principle of Utility Theory (von Neumann and Morgenstern, 1947). It is proposed that simple decisions can be made by calculating the utility of possible outcomes and choosing the highest. The expected utility can be calculated with the following formula:

Expected utility = (probability of outcome) × (utility of outcome)

It's not always possible to know the probability of something occurring or how much it is worth (this might seem quite abstract and strange). Savage (1954) extended this idea by suggesting that probabilities and utilities used to calculate expected utility may be subjective, giving us Subjective Expected Utility theory (or SEU).

To understand what this all means, it is sometimes useful to work with an example. Imagine you are choosing between reading this section of the book and skipping to the summary. If it is crossing your mind, then you will be weighing up your options. You may be thinking about what you would gain from continuing reading (the outcome), how likely that is (probability of outcome) and how much that means to you (subjective utility of outcome). Let's assume that if you continue reading this section, you will learn something about decision making. You are a bit tired so you think there is a 50:50 chance that some of it will sink in (0.5 probability of achieving the outcome) and that if you had to rate it out of 100 (with 100 the highest possible value), then learning something about decision making is about 80 for you. This is our subjective utility. We can then plug these numbers into the equation:

Expected utility = 0.5 × 80 = 40

So our subjective expected utility of learning something about decision making by reading this section is 40. Essentially this is a random number until we introduce a useful comparison. Imagine that you skip straight to the summary instead. Now the chance of you learning something by just looking at the summary may be closer to 10:90 (that is, a 0.1 probability of achieving the outcome) and the subjective value of this remains the same (about 80). We can then look again at the equation and see that:

Expected utility = 0.1 × 80 = 8

So our subjective expected utility of learning something about decision making by skipping to the summary is 8. The theory goes that, having worked out these values, you should always choose the option that will bring you the highest expected utility. In this example the expected utility of continuing to read this section (40) is greater than the expected utility of skipping to the summary (8), therefore continuing to read this section is the best choice if you want to learn something about decision making.

Task —— Think of a decision you make on a regular basis. Calculate subjective expected utilities in the same manner as the example in the text. Compare the values that you calculate. In real life, do you always choose the option that your calculations suggest you should?

Some limitations of this approach may already be clear to you. For example, there may be a number of **variables** that also have an influence. While finishing this chapter has a high expected utility, you may have to miss a party, which will obviously lower it. A simple decision analysis can include these possibilities, if you like, but you might need to think of all the possible consequences (and that is no easy task). Things might also change over time – you may find that the subjective utility changes as you get more tired or as your house burns down around you.

Nowadays, analyses like this are used more to stimulate thought and discussion about options than as a way of finding a 100 per cent correct 'answer'. While normative theories provide some interesting ideas for how decisions should be made (to maximise utility), a more interesting question is how decisions are actually made.

Descriptive theories

Although useful, normative theories do not account for other influences on decision making, such as the amount of information available, how it is presented and the type of decision it is. One theoretical account that begins to provide this more descriptive analysis is Prospect Theory (Kahneman and Tversky, 1979).

In Prospect Theory, outcomes of decisions are considered as having gains or losses rather than utilities. These gains or losses can be referred to as 'prospects' (hence Prospect Theory). The exact gains and losses for each decision depend upon how it is viewed (or represented). The theory suggests that we begin by mentally discarding information that is of little use for making the decision. We then use a neutral reference point from which to judge potential gains or losses. The prospects of the decision are then evaluated according to the individual person's attitude towards risk. Research into this theory has highlighted two interesting features of human decision making, among others:

- loss aversion;

- framing effects.

Each of these is discussed in turn.

Loss aversion

A central idea in Prospect Theory is that people 'feel' losses more than they 'feel' gains. In more formal terms, losses have a greater impact on preferences when making decisions than gains of an equivalent value (Kahneman and Tversky, 1979; Tversky and Kahneman, 1981). Let's think about this using an example first provided by Tversky and Kahneman (1981). They gave 150 people the following scenario and two choices.

Imagine that you face the following pair of decisions at the same time. First examine both decisions, then indicate the options you prefer.

Decision (i). Choose between:
A.   a sure gain of $240;
B.   25% chance to gain $1000, and 75% chance to gain nothing.

Decision (ii). Choose between:
A.   a sure loss of $750;
B.   75% chance to lose $1000, and 25% chance to lose nothing.

What decisions did you make? If you haven't made your own decision, then please go back and do so. We'll look first at decision (i). Tversky and Kahneman (1981) found that of the 150 people they asked, 84 per cent chose option A – a sure gain of $240. People were unwilling to take a risk for a higher amount because there was the chance they would not gain anything (loss aversion). Responses to decision (ii) showed the opposite pattern. Only 13 per cent chose a sure loss of $750, instead choosing to gamble on a 75 per cent chance of losing $1000, with a 25 per cent chance of losing nothing. Respondents were therefore willing to take a gamble when it came to losses. This is because people 'feel' losses much more than they 'feel' gains.

Task ⌐   In your own words, describe what is meant by loss aversion. Generate a new example that illustrates your thoughts.

Loss aversion is an important phenomenon as it illustrates a key difference between normative and descriptive theories. Normative theories predict that gains and losses of equal size will be treated in similar ways. This fits the 'rational' model of humans as mathematical decision makers, and maybe some people are. However, loss aversion demonstrates that gains and losses of equal size aren't treated in the same way – it clearly demonstrates one limitation to considering humans as completely rational and mathematical decision makers. The differences are even more evident when you consider the powerful effects of presenting decisions in different ways.

Framing effects

How you present a decision can have startling effects on the preferences that people have. Loss aversion is a good example of these framing effects: if you frame a decision in terms of losses, people may be more willing to take a risk than if you frame it in terms of gains. This is only one example of a framing effect. Many experiments have been reported by Kahneman and Tversky, among others, to illustrate this point. Here is just one more example taken from Tversky and Kahneman (1981). This one is about going to see a play: different people were presented with different scenarios, but essentially the same decision. Let's start with scenario one.

> Imagine that you have decided to see a play where admission is $10 per ticket. As you enter the theatre you discover that you have lost a $10 bill. Would you still pay $10 for a ticket for the play?

Tversky and Kahneman (1981) posed this problem to 183 people and found that 88 per cent – the vast majority of them – responded that they would still pay for a ticket for the play. This would mean that they would be down $20 in total – let's bear this in mind when we look at scenario two.

> Imagine that you have decided to see a play and paid the admission price of $10 per ticket. As you enter the theatre you discover that you have lost the ticket. Would you pay $10 for another ticket?

This problem was posed to 200 people and it was found that less than half (46 per cent) stated that they would pay for another ticket. Remember that in the first scenario 88 per cent said they would still buy a ticket if they had just lost the money. Both scenarios involve being down $20 and both involve getting to see the play (if 'yes' is chosen). Yet people were more or less willing to pay for the ticket depending upon how the decision was framed. Tversky and Kahneman (1981) suggested that people may have different 'mental accounts'. In the first scenario, the money was lost from separate mental accounts so the losses felt smaller. In the second scenario the $20 came from the same 'account', which made the loss feel larger. Hence people were willing to buy the ticket in the first scenario because 'mental accounting' meant that the loss was not felt in the same way.

Task — In your own words, describe the difference between normative theories of decision making and descriptive theories of decision making. Use examples of either loss aversion or framing effects to illustrate your thoughts.

Psychological aspects of decision making, such as the influence of framing, produce results that are not easily explained by simple rational models. It is clear that humans do not make decisions in the precise mathematical way that normative theories suggest. Research suggests that there are a number of rules of thumb (heuristics) and biases that determine how decisions are made.

Skill builder activity

Influencing decision making

Transferable skill focus: problem solving

Key question: *How can our knowledge of human decision making be used when selling something?*

You have learned about two key ideas in Prospect Theory: loss aversion and framing effects. Choose one of these two ideas and try to solve the following problem using them.

We are going to pretend that someone has come to you, as a psychologist, and asked for your help with negotiating the sale of some textbooks they have been given. Some of the books aren't in great condition, and your friend is worried that the books will not sell, or at least not for a very good price. You are determined to use what you have learned about loss aversion and framing effects to help your friend negotiate. Ideally, they want as high a price as they can get for the books. Review the material presented above, and think about how these ideas could be used to help your friend.

In 500 words, write down how your friend should present the books to give them the best possible chance of selling at a relatively high price. For example, consider how they could be framed to spread the cost across different 'mental accounts' or how the product could be presented to emphasise 'gains'. You may find some inspiration by looking at how products are sold in the real world.

Skill builder review

This activity helps develop your problem-solving skills, focusing on your ability to use broad information to answer a much more specific question, and to transfer what you have learned in one domain to another. This is an important skill because information is rarely presented in a way that answers the very specific question (or problem) you are interested in. The activity encourages you to practise transferring your knowledge from one area to another, as well as reflecting on and critically thinking about these aspects of decision making.

Other skills you may have used in this activity include: critical thinking; comparison; decision making; and reflection.

Heuristics and bias

There have been many investigations into the heuristics and biases that we use when making decisions, and a large amount of experimental evidence has been gathered. 'Representativeness' and 'availability' are two important ideas from this body of research.

Representativeness

Earlier in this chapter we discussed how people categorise things. It was argued that the more accurate approaches to understanding how we do this are ones that take into account how typical something is of the relevant concept or category. We thought about this in terms of family resemblances, the notion that there is a set of particular characteristics with different weights that determine if something belongs to a category or not. This idea of representativeness is also important when we think about decision making.

Imagine the following scenario: you are out walking with a friend and you find two lottery tickets. Both of the tickets are for the lottery draw that evening. You decide to take one ticket each. Your friend kindly says that *you* can decide which of the two tickets you want to keep. One ticket has the numbers 1, 2, 3, 4, 5, 6. The other ticket has the numbers 5, 18, 19, 31, 35, 45. Which ticket would you choose to keep? Statistically, both tickets have an equal probability of winning. In the decision-making literature this is known as the 'base-rate information': the probability that certain events or outcomes will occur. The base-rate information tells us that it doesn't matter which ticket you choose because they both have the same chance of winning. However, many people would choose the second ticket over the first. Why is this? One suggestion is we view the second ticket to be more representative of a winning lottery ticket. That is, you ignore the fact that they both have an equal chance (the base-rate information) and instead make the decision on the basis of how 'like' a winning ticket you think it is (the representativeness heuristic).

Task — Describe the representativeness heuristic in your own terms. Generate an example from your own life experiences to illustrate your thoughts.

The idea that we make decisions based on how typical we think something is, rather than exact probabilities, was first formally introduced by Kahneman and Tversky (1973). Around the same time they also introduced another heuristic called the availability heuristic.

Availability

The lottery example above has some very specific properties. For example, we know the exact probability of the lottery tickets being winning tickets. However, many decisions are made when this sort of information is not available.

For example, you may consider buying a top but are worried whether your friends will like it. You do not know the exact probability of them liking the top, and you would have to go to some effort to find out. One strategy you might use is to think of similar tops and the comments your friends have made about them. If you can think of lots of recent examples where they have said they like similar tops, then you will probably decide to buy it. In contrast, if you can think of a few examples in the past where they have liked such tops, but a very recent example of them saying they hated a similar top, then you may be less likely to buy it.

In the example above, your decision may not be determined by knowledge of exact probabilities but instead by how easily you can bring similar examples to mind. This is how the term 'availability' is used when psychologists are talking about decision making. Tversky and Kahneman (1973) suggested that the ease with which examples come to mind influences judgements we make about how often events occur.

Adaptive thinking

The evidence underpinning the above ideas focused on how people make decisions that are logically incorrect (according to normative theories). Gigerenzer and colleagues have put forward a different perspective on these issues. Gigerenzer and Goldstein (1996) argued that we use these heuristics because they are actually useful. This is different from the idea that we use them because we are not capable of doing anything else. It is suggested that these heuristics – described variously as being 'fast and frugal heuristics' or 'one-reason heuristics' – are used because they produce a satisfactory decision (rather than a perfect one). As with much of this research, an example is probably useful. Try to answer the following questions:

- Which city has the largest population, Birmingham or Manchester?

- Which city has the smallest population, Manchester or Wilberfoss?

You may have struggled more with the first question than with the second question. Is it because you know the exact population of Manchester and the exact population of Wilberfoss, but not that of Birmingham? Unless you know a lot about the East Riding of Yorkshire, that probably isn't the reason. You might not even have heard of Wilberfoss, but if you have been in the UK long enough, you will have heard of Manchester and therefore opted for it when making your second decision. The first decision is not as easy because you probably recognise both Manchester and Birmingham as big cities. This idea of making a decision on the basis of 'recognising one of them' is known as the 'recognition heuristic', and it is argued that a lot of the time this heuristic can produce correct answers. The implication is that we don't need a lot of accurate information to make some decisions (such as judging relative populations). Recognising something when you don't recognise what you are judging it against can often lead you to a correct decision.

To continue our example, according to the 2001 UK census there were 1,855 people living in Wilberfoss and 392,819 living in Manchester. The fact that you may not recognise Wilberfoss is related to the fact that it has quite a small population. So not recognising it, or not knowing much about it, is a useful way to have made the decision. Goldstein and Gigerenzer (2002) did a similar experiment to our **thought experiment**. One of the questions they asked was 'Which has the largest population, San Diego or San Antonio?' They found that around two-thirds of Americans correctly decided that San Diego is larger than San Antonio. When the same question was given to a group of Germans, they all made the correct decision, at least partially because they recognised San Diego 'more'.

Task ── In 500 words, write down what is unique and important about the adaptive thinking perspective adopted by Gigerenzer and colleagues. You may find it useful to include an example to illustrate your thoughts.

The extent to which all the available evidence supports the use of these heuristics is an ongoing debate (see Newell and Shanks, 2004), yet it is clear that fast and frugal heuristics do, under some circumstances, play a useful role. Indeed, Gigerenzer and Brighton (2009) argue that is the most **ecologically valid** explanation of how humans make decisions.

What you have learned in this chapter is only a broad overview of the ideas that exist on these topics. We have focused on classic ideas and studies as this may be the first time you have ever sat down and begun to really think about this in detail. Together, these ideas and studies are just the very beginnings of what are still rapidly expanding areas of research. Interesting questions are being asked about different aspects such as the number and type of heuristics that might exist, how concepts are learned and how we might classify the types of problems that are solved. If you find these topics interesting, then there are many more approaches, problems, theories and solutions that are worthy of your time.

Assignments

1. Compare and contrast the classical, exemplar and prototype approaches to concepts and categories. Construct three new examples that illustrate the major differences between these approaches, and use these examples to argue which approach provides the best-fitting model of how we construct concepts and categories, explaining your reasoning.

2. Evaluate the limitations of studying problem solving in a laboratory setting. Think of some advantages and disadvantages of studying problem solving in this way, and some advantages and disadvantages of studying problem solving in 'real world' environments. Provide an argument for which environment allows for the more accurate research findings, and give your reasoning why.

3. Given the advantages and disadvantages of theories of decision making, which approach (normative or descriptive) would be best when someone decides who to vote for in the general election? Clearly state why you think a certain approach should be used and defend the reasoning for your judgement.

Summary: what you have learned

In this chapter you have learned that how we mentally represent concepts is important and you have been made aware of a number of different approaches to understanding this, including: classical approaches that suggest concepts are constructed through lists of defining attributes; prototype approaches that suggest people make judgements on how typical something is in comparison to a prototype; and exemplar approaches that suggest judgements are made on the basis of previous instances in memory. In addition, we have considered specific features of the available evidence such as the effects of context or the influence of past experiences.

You have also learned how cognitive psychologists have studied problem solving. You will remember that *Gestalt* psychologists argued that problem solving relies on more than trial and error, suggesting insight as a key feature of how problems are solved. It has also been suggested that analogies may play an important role in these insight experiences. You have learned that considerable progress has been made in this area through comparing the brain with a computer. From this work we have learned that checking the difference between where you are (current state) and where you want to be (goals/sub-goals) is considered an important feature of good problem solving.

Finally, you have learned about the psychology of decision making. You are now aware that early theories of decision making were largely mathematical and descriptive, focusing on 'ideal' answers to hypothetical problems. You have learned that humans make decisions in ways that these models can't predict, and that this is captured in descriptive theories that include ideas such as loss aversion and framing effects. You have also learned about additional heuristics such as representativeness and availability, which act as mental 'rules of thumb' when making decisions. Recent arguments have been presented that suggest that these heuristics should not be viewed as limitations but instead as examples of how we can make useful decisions in simpler ways.

You have also had the opportunity in this chapter to improve your skills in analysis and evaluation. You have learned that evaluation is not just about highlighting negative things but also about careful consideration of the balance between positive and negative aspects. In evaluating theories, you have learned that important aspects to consider are whether the theory explains the research evidence, if the ideas in the theory are precise and clearly explained, and if it is clear how to interpret evidence using the theory. It is important to note that there are many more criteria than just these.

You have also learned a bit about your skills as a problem solver. You have learned that it is a skill that often involves working from where you are to what you would like to achieve, step by step. Problem solving can involve a number of different strategies, and regularly involves taking knowledge you have learned about one thing and applying it to your very specific problem.

Further reading

Davidson, JE and Sternberg, RE (eds) (2003) *The psychology of problem solving*. Cambridge: Cambridge University Press.

This excellent edition provides a more detailed summary of key theoretical positions and experimental findings in the psychology of problem solving.

Gigerenzer, G, Hertwig, R and Pachur, T (eds) (2011) *Fast and frugal heuristics: theories, tests and applications*. Oxford: Oxford University Press.

This edited collection provides an important reference work for the use of fast and frugal heuristics across many real-world and applied domains, in addition to reporting and summarising more theoretical and experimental advances in this area.

Mareschal, D, Quinn, PC and Lea, SEG (eds) (2010) *The making of human concepts*. Oxford: Oxford University Press.

This exciting book draws together the views of prominent cognitive psychologists alongside those of developmental psychologists and comparative psychologists to try to answer the question 'What, if anything, is unique about human concepts?'

Chapter 3

Learning and memory

Learning outcomes

By the end of this chapter you should:

- be able to describe two theoretical approaches to understanding memory;

- be able to discuss the relationship between encoding and retrieval;

- be able to analyse what factors may lead to forgetting or false memories; and

- be able to reflect upon the personal assumptions you are making about memory, as well as learning how to support your independent learning through the development of research maps.

Introduction

Sometimes we can forget how important learning and memory are. Whether it involves learning about ideas before taking an exam, physically learning how to drive, or learning how to cope with an awkward relative, learning runs through everything that we do. We use our memory all the time every single day, from remembering that it is milk that goes on cereal in the morning to remembering where we live and how to get there in the evening. In this chapter we will discuss a number of classic studies and important theories in the topic area of learning and memory. We will first look at how people have tried to understand memory in a very broad sense. We will consider one important part of learning, the encoding and retrieval context, before learning about what failures in learning and memory can tell us about the mind. Before we get to that stage we need to think about what a theory of memory should look like.

Accounts of memory

Research on learning and memory has been a particularly fruitful area, with lots of time and money spent on it. We can only guess why, but it is possible that part of this popularity comes from how easy it is to test learning and memory both inside a laboratory and outside in the real world. A simple memory test can be put together with a list of words and people who agree to take part. Experiments can be easily made in which the influence of many different things can be explored (e.g. type of words on the test, size of the test, delay before remembering them, how it is presented). The result is that lots of different exciting aspects of human memory have been studied, described and predicted. While there are many different accounts, cognitive psychologists can be broadly classified as adopting one of two approaches:

- a structural approach;

- a processing approach.

You will learn about the main assumptions of both of these approaches.

Structural approaches

A structural approach to understanding the psychology of memory is one that focuses on identifying different types of memory and working out the relationships between them. The main assumption with much of this work is that memory is not one thing but a combination of different 'types' of memory. A few examples should make this clear.

Atkinson and Shiffrin (1968) developed a model of memory that argued for a sequence of three different types of memory, also called mental stores. They argued that memory had a specific structure that consisted of both stores and processes that were 'fixed'. They also argued that there were a number of processes that were more flexible than these stores that participants could use at will to influence their own memories (such as mentally rehearsing information). Most attention has been paid to the three separate stores they proposed, which were: a sensory register; a short-term store; and a long-term store. Indeed, you may already be familiar with the terms 'short-term memory' and 'long-term memory' from everyday use.

The sensory register was put forward as a system that receives its information from the environment, and is the closest link to the information we get from our senses. It was believed that information exists in this sensory register for a very brief period of time before being lost. If information is relevant, it is selectively 'copied' into the short-term store. Information is still lost from the short-term store, but it is a little more permanent than the sensory register. They estimated that information is lost from this short-term store in about 30 seconds unless rehearsed. It was argued that if the information is needed on an even more permanent basis, then it is 'copied' into the long-term store. This suggests that everything goes in one direction (from sensory register to short-term store to long-term store). However, Atkinson and Shiffrin (1968) also suggested that information can be copied from the long-term store into the short-term store if it is needed. This flow of information through the system is illustrated in Figure 3.1.

There is not enough space here to evaluate all of the research and evidence that is relevant to this basic model, but it is possible to pick out some aspects that can begin to make up our idea of a structural approach to understanding memory. In particular, it is important to note that it is not believed that there is just one memory system. This assumption underpins the idea that if there is

Figure 3.1: *Flow of information through memory as described by Atkinson and Shiffrin (1968)*

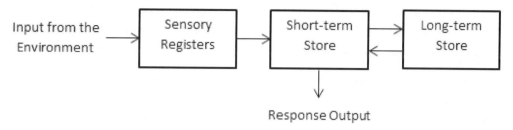

Response Output

not just one system, then we must try to understand the different systems that do exist and how they are related. A few more examples should help you understand this.

Long-term memory

The long-term store, as labelled by Atkinson and Shiffrin (1968), is now more commonly known as long-term memory. Squire (1992) suggested that this long-term memory system could best be understood by thinking about a number of differences. One distinction is between **explicit memory** and **implicit memory**.

Explicit memory is, broadly speaking, memory for facts and events. Remembering that London is the capital city of England is an example of remembering an explicit fact. Remembering what it was like the first time you visited London, how you felt when you first got on the Underground and how you felt when you first stepped into Leicester Square are all explicit memories of specific episodes (episodic memories). Indeed, this is a second distinction, which is drawn within explicit memory: **semantic memory** and **episodic memory** (Tulving, 1972). Memory for knowledge of the world, separate from specific one-off events, is known as semantic memory; for example, you know that a tomato (depending on ripeness) is generally red. In comparison, episodic memory is memory for a very specific single episode or event, such as when you first saw a tomato, or when you first visited London.

In contrast to explicit memory, implicit memory is more closely related to learning without being aware what you are learning. For example, you may be remembering information that you encountered earlier on to help complete a task right now, but not be aware that you are doing so. A key distinction between the two ideas is therefore the level of awareness related to each of them.

Short-term memory

Just as it has been suggested that long-term memory can be divided into different systems, a similar approach has been taken with the short-term store, also referred to as short-term memory. The most influential structural model is that of the working memory model (Baddeley and Hitch, 1974).

An important aspect of this model is that it aimed not only to theorise about temporary storage of information but also to focus on how the system is used during complex cognitive activity such as thought and reasoning. That is why it is known as the 'working' memory model, because it looks at how the stored information is put to work.

The other important feature of the working memory model, for our purposes, is that a very specific structure was proposed. It was suggested that working memory could be divided into: a phono-logical loop; a visuo-spatial sketchpad; and a central executive. In broad terms, the phonological loop was proposed as a system that could store a small amount of information in a 'speech-based' form. The visuo-spatial sketchpad was described as an equivalent of the phonological loop that could instead store information based on visual characteristics (visual) and relative position in space (spatial). The purpose of the final component, the central executive, was described as to control and co-ordinate mental activities (such as reasoning) that needed to use the information in these separate short-term stores. It was argued that the central executive was limited by the number of 'resources' it had. The suggestion was that these 'resources' could be used up for either storage of information or other processes, as was necessary according to what the person was doing. This proposed structure is illustrated in Figure 3.2.

Figure 3.2: *Structure of working memory as proposed by Baddeley and Hitch (1974)*

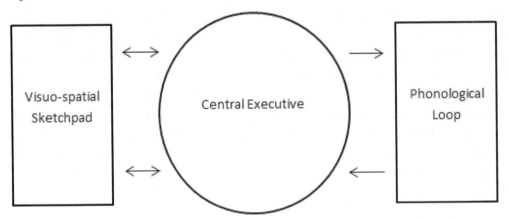

There has been over 35 years of research and development of this original concept of working memory and it would be impossible to learn about all of it here. However, it is most notable that the purpose of this model is to map out distinctions between different 'types' of processes and different types of information. This is a key aspect of a structural approach to memory.

Processing approaches

You have learned that a main assumption of a structural approach is that memory should be researched in terms of different stores or systems, and the relationships between them. While there have been lots of cognitive psychologists who have researched memory from this perspective, there is an alternative that is put forward by some other psychologists. These other psychologists argue that there is no need to think about memory in terms of different systems, because memory can be explained in terms of the *same* system but with different processes (e.g. Nairne, 1990; Neath and Surprenant, 2003).

Levels of processing

An early example of a processing approach to memory was provided by Craik and Lockhart (1972), who proposed a 'levels of processing' account. The basic idea of this account was that anything we perceive undergoes a certain amount of mental processing. Some things get processed only at what you might call a 'shallow' level; for example, someone might say something to you and you hear the sounds but don't really get the meaning. Alternatively, information may get processed at a 'deep' level; for example, as someone tells you something you may try to work out their meaning and intention, thinking about what they might or might not know already, and what you might or might not know already, and how it all links together.

The general idea is that the level of processing (how deep or shallow it is) is more important than ideas such as different memory stores. Hence a memory lasts a long time and is very clear in your mind because you have processed it in a deep way, not necessarily because it was copied into a long-term 'store'.

It is possible to find many criticisms of this approach, and Craik and Lockhart (1990) have responded to many of them in a revised proposal. Perhaps the most important to consider when developing your critical thinking skills is demonstrated with a thought experiment.

How do we know what constitutes deep processing? Let's assume you have the belief that trying to work out a rhyme for a word will result in deep processing of that word. You might test this by asking participants in one version of the experiment to think of rhymes for words, and asking participants in another version of the experiment simply to look at the words. You could then see how many words they remember. If participants who have been trying to think of rhymes remember more words, then you might conclude that rhyming words have led to deeper processing. Now, something that you have to be very careful about when evaluating ideas is to make sure that there is no **circular reasoning**. Let me demonstrate by simplifying even further the reasoning for the above thought: deep processing leads to better memory; memory was better, therefore the processing was deep. The argument is circular with the word 'deep' merely acting as a substitute for 'better memory'. This problem emerges because it is not possible to define precisely what 'deep' processing is; this in turn makes the account descriptive of the results that have been found, but it is difficult to make predictions using it.

Obviously, this does not represent all of the finer points of the levels of a processing approach, and there is plenty more to learn about it, and other processing approaches, if you find this alternative interesting.

You might like to know that while we learn about differences between structural approaches and processing approaches, many cognitive psychologists, such as Baddeley (1982), argue that this is simply looking at the same thing but from a different perspective. Indeed, the structural approach does not exclude processing but instead considers it to be an important part of many of the models proposed. The sticking point is whether there is a single memory system or multiple systems.

Task — In your own words, summarise the main differences between a structural approach to memory and a processing approach to memory. Use examples to illustrate your ideas.

Critical thinking activity

What is memory?

Critical thinking focus: reflection

Key question: *Is memory a set of separate systems or separate processes?*

As you have learned, cognitive psychologists disagree as to how we should understand and explore memory: some researchers support a view of distinct memory systems, while others believe memory can be completely understood in terms of different processes. In this activity you will practise a skill known as reflection. Broadly speaking, reflection is when you think in depth about your experiences, action, feelings and responses to them in a way that you might not usually do.

In this activity reflect upon the claims cognitive psychologists make about how we should understand and explore memory. It is important for this activity that you have read the section of this chapter titled 'Accounts of memory'. If you have not done so, or not done so recently, then please read the section before continuing this activity.

Think back on your experience of reading about the different ways of understanding memory. Then try to answer the following questions.

What did you think at the time? Did one approach seem 'naturally' correct to you?

How did you feel about the approaches? Would you need more evidence to be convinced of a particular approach compared to the other? Why?

Think deeply about these reflections and try to understand what these mean for how *you* think about memory. Try to answer the question 'What are your personal assumptions about how memory works?'

Critical thinking review

This activity helps develop your reflection skills while thinking about the nature of memory. In particular, this activity gives you an opportunity to step back and be aware of the assumptions that you are introducing to your own understanding of what is being presented. This is very important because we often suffer from something known as **confirmation bias**. This is when we easily accept ideas that are similar to our own, and are less willing to believe ideas that we don't agree with. Being able to stand back and reflect on your own views is an important step in recognising when your understanding may have been clouded by confirmation bias.

In science it is very important that we do everything we can to avoid this bias. For example, we have to be careful that we don't just focus on those findings that support our arguments or ignore findings that don't fit what we believe. This can be very difficult, and good reflection skills are very important for overcoming this bias.

Other skills you may have used in this activity include: analysing and evaluating; and comparison.

Thankfully, there are a number of different ideas about memory that can be understood without having to decide if information is stored and processed in a single memory system or multiple systems. We will now look at just three of those: retrieval of memories; forgetting information; and falsely remembering.

Retrieval

Have you ever tried to remember something that you know you should know and yet just can't remember it? For example, have you ever watched a film and recognised in it somewhere you have been, but failed to remember where that was and what you were doing there? Or have you ever recognised the face of someone in the street but struggled to remember how, or why, you know them? We often describe this as having something on the 'tip of our tongue' but it is obviously more to do with our mind than anything else. Interestingly, we often find that a simple bit of related information can suddenly result in our being able to remember everything we wanted to know, breaking us free from the 'tip of the tongue' feeling. In this section we will learn about how the spreading activation account of memory is used to explain this phenomenon, and we will look at the close relationship between encoding and retrieval in explaining how and when we are able to remember things.

Spreading activation theory

We have already suggested that getting some additional information can mean that you suddenly remember something you've been struggling to recall. This bit of 'reminder' information is known as a 'cue' in cognitive psychology. The importance of cues comes from the idea that memories are represented in our minds in a way that they are associated together. That is to say, a memory for a face may be associated with many other memories, such as your mood the last time you saw that face, what you were doing at the time, and where you were. All of these memories are linked in the sense that your memory for where you were last Tuesday may be linked to a face of someone with you, just as your memory for that face is linked to some information about how you felt.

Now this may sound obvious, but it is important to consider alternative ways that our memories could be stored. One way to imagine them being stored is to imagine every memory being locked in a box, such as a safe, put in a drawer or zipped up as a file on a computer. This is a literal form of storage, and what is interesting is that how we store memories in our minds is much cleverer than that.

Some cognitive psychologists talk about these links between information in memory as having different 'strengths', so there are strong links and weak links in what you might think of as an incredibly large and complicated web of memories. The idea is that when we try to remember something we take advantage of this web so that we can remember something indirectly through different links, rather than remembering it directly. For example, you may struggle to recall the capital city of Norway until I remind you that it rhymes with slow, or that it begins with O. Some cognitive psychologists suggest that these links and memories can have different levels of activation. If some information has high levels of activation, then we are likely to be able to consciously remember it (retrieve it), while if it has low levels of activation, then we are much less likely to be able to remember it.

We can use this theory to begin to understand how a cue works. One suggestion is that a cue, or many cues, increases the activation through the activation 'spreading'. To continue our example above, by giving you the information of 'Norway', 'rhymes with slow' and 'starts with an O', the memory that the capital city of Norway is 'Oslo' becomes highly activated because of its links to these ideas. The links between these bits of information mean that the activation 'spreads' to the thing we are trying to remember, resulting in the conscious experience of being able to remember the information. This is known as a spreading activation account of retrieval from memory (e.g. Anderson, 1983) and is a useful way to think about why cues can be so effective. However, the effectiveness of cues can differ. An important idea that guides how effective cues are is the encoding specificity principle.

The encoding specificity principle

Throughout this book we will continue to learn about the importance of context to many different aspects of cognition. Context in simple terms is the environment or setting in which an event occurs. For example, if at school you learned to speak French or Spanish in the same room for a whole year, then that room is part of the context. Similarly, if you see a crime in a particular street at a particular time of day, then these things are part of the context too. These examples are of aspects of the setting that are external to you, and can sometimes be known as the **extrinsic context**. However, there is also such a thing as an **intrinsic context**. For example, the mood you were in when you learned a particular word in French may be part of the internal context. Alternatively, what you were thinking about when you witnessed a crime might also be part of the internal context. A context can therefore be very broad and takes into account lots of things at that moment in time.

It has been argued that the context when you learn something, or experience something, is very important when you come to remember it later on. The process of taking something 'on board' as a memory is known as the encoding process, and it is suggested that every memory does not sit alone but is instead stored with its context (Tulving and Osler, 1968). More specifically, the encoding specificity principle states that a cue will be an effective way of prompting retrieval if, and only if, it was encoded with this relevant cue information during learning.

A classic example of this principle can be found in a study by Godden and Baddeley (1975). They tested the memories of deep sea divers in the following way. The divers listened to a list of 40 unrelated words in the knowledge that they would have to try to recall them shortly afterwards. Some of their participants listened to them while on a beach, while some of them listened to them under ten feet of water. Being on the beach, and being underwater, created the different contexts when the lists were encoded.

Godden and Baddeley (1975) then tested their participants to see how many words they could remember. They did this by asking them to say them out loud. They left some of their participants in the same context: people on the beach recalled the words on the beach; and people in the water recalled the words in the water. For these participants the external context at retrieval was therefore physically similar to the external context at encoding. The remaining participants had to recall the words in the environment they had *not* learned them in: people who learned on the beach recalled underwater; and people that learned underwater recalled on the beach. In this case the retrieval context was different from the encoding context. Godden and Baddeley (1975) found that the number of words correctly recalled was much higher when the encoding context and the retrieval context were the same, compared to when they were different.

Interestingly, Godden and Baddeley (1980) repeated their experiment but instead of asking the divers to recall the words out loud, they asked them to identify them from lists of words they may have possibly seen. This is known as a recognition test, rather than recall, and it is interesting to learn that when recognising words the similarity in context was not important. Seeing the words written down was a much stronger cue than anything the environment could have provided.

In terms of 'real world' experiences the implication is that if you want to recall as much as possible, you should study in similar conditions to how you may be tested. This may not always be possible, so you may be pleased to learn that analyses suggest that even imagining the context at retrieval can help (Smith and Vela, 2001). However, this is less likely to be important if you are completing a 'multiple choice' exam where you are given the options to choose from.

While we have focused here on just one main example, that of changing the physical environment, other cognitive psychologists have found similar results while looking at the mood at encoding and retrieval (e.g. Eich et al., 1994), as well as the physiological state (Miles and Hardman, 1998). There have even been suggestions that something as simple as chewing gum is enough to aid context-dependent improvements in memory (Baker et al., 2004), although this finding has been challenged by other researchers (Miles and Johnson, 2007).

Retrieval in the real world

Throughout this section we have learned about encoding and retrieval by thinking about examples such as learning a language or taking an exam. You may also recognise an application of these ideas in how police try to solve crimes. Sometimes the police will reconstruct a crime using actors. They will then ask witnesses, or victims, to watch the events. By re-staging the crime in the same place, at the same time of day, but with actors, the police are attempting to re-create the environmental cues. The hope is that the re-staging will externally cue people to recall important details. It is possible that the re-creation will also bring about similar intrinsic cues (e.g. fear, apprehension) but in a safe environment. You will know from what you have learned here that because of how the mind works, providing all of these cues can often help people to remember more than if they were just asked questions.

If a reconstruction of a crime is not possible, police may also use cognitive interviews (e.g. Geiselman et al. 1985). The questions in a cognitive interview are specifically designed to help participants mentally re-create the context. You have already learned that this mental re-creation of context is known to help with the retrieval of relevant memories. This is a simple demonstration of how knowledge created through research in cognitive psychology has been applied in a 'real world' situation (solving a crime).

Task ⎯ Generate another example from the 'real world' where you think accurate retrieval of memories is important. Describe how what you have learned here could be used to help people in your example accurately remember.

Forgetting

As important as remembering is to our daily lives, it is easy to overlook the impact that forgetting has. Indeed, we might often underestimate how much we actually forget. For example, can you remember what the weather was like one week ago? Back in 1895 Cattell asked this of his students. In reality it had snowed, although it had cleared up by the time he was asking them. He found that 49 of the 56 students failed to mention the snow.

Given how much, and how quickly, we forget, there is obviously lots we can learn about the mind from this simple experience. We will focus here on two important questions about the nature of forgetting.

- How fast do we forget?

- Why does it happen?

Speed of forgetting

Some of the earliest work in the field of memory was not concerned with just how memories are stored or retrieved but instead on how quickly we forget. The classic study in this area was reported by Ebbinghaus (1885, 1913). Like many early psychologists, Ebbinghaus used himself as the only participant. He set himself the task of learning a set of 169 separate lists of 13 nonsense syllables then relearned each set after a short period of time, from 21 minutes up to 31 days. As you might expect, Ebbinghaus couldn't always remember all of the nonsense syllables in the lists. As his measure of forgetting, he took the time needed to learn the list again. What he found was that forgetting occurred very quickly at first, but after this very quick period of forgetting there was relatively little further forgetting. In other words, memories that made it past this initial period were more stable over long periods of time.

Task ⎯ The next time there is particularly bad weather (lots of snowfall, high winds or torrential rain), make a note of the weather conditions, perhaps in a diary. A week later ask friends and family what the weather had been like on that day. You may be surprised at how easily it is forgotten!

One obvious limitation to this research (and much that followed) is that we don't spend much time learning lists of nonsense syllables. When research looks at something that is not part of many people's common experience, it is referred to as lacking **ecological validity**. This lack of ecological validity is a limitation of much of the research in cognitive psychology that relies on laboratory experiments. You have already learned that cognitive psychology places a great deal of importance on collecting its evidence in a scientific way. Part of this method is to control for as many things that could vary as possible, trying to ensure that the only thing that varies in the experiment is the thing(s) you are interested in (independent variable(s)) and what you are measuring (dependent variable(s)). Because most situations in life are not as controlled as this, the importance of careful experimenting in cognitive psychology makes ecological validity a major concern for this area. A key assumption with some research in cognitive psychology is therefore that the principles and theories that are based on laboratory experiments *will* apply to our everyday lives, or at the very least that they don't need to apply directly in order to be worth researching.

In terms of forgetting, there is interesting evidence to suggest that what has been found in the laboratory can also be found in more ecologically valid situations. For example, Bahrick and Phelps (1987) took advantage of an annual reunion event at their university to investigate forgetting of different things that the students might have learned when they were originally studying there. One of these things was their memory for Spanish that had been learned as a foreign language. Like Ebbinghaus before them, they found that there was a rapid period of forgetting of participants' knowledge of Spanish (in this case two years) that was followed by a much longer period of relatively little forgetting (up to 50 years). The initial laboratory findings of Ebbinghaus therefore apply to experience in the real world, confirming that the ideas are ecologically valid.

It is worth noting that what you have just learned about, the speed of forgetting, can also depend upon the type of thing that is being forgotten. For example, there are suggestions that very specific skills, such as flying skills, are rarely forgotten over a two-year period (Fleishman and Parker, 1962) while other skills, such as medical resuscitation skills, can be rapidly forgotten over the first year since learning (McKenna and Glendon, 1985).

Theories of forgetting

Having learned that forgetting often occurs very rapidly before a period of relative stability, it is important that we start to think about *why* forgetting occurs.

If we think about this for a minute, we are likely to come up with at least one of two potential ideas about why forgetting occurs: the first is that forgetting occurs because memories naturally fade over time (also called 'decay' or 'trace decay'); the second is that forgetting occurs because other things happen that interact or interfere with information you could remember (known as 'interference'). These are two of the main ideas that have been explored by cognitive psychologists.

Part of the difficulty of finding evidence to support either of these two ideas on their own is that time and events are always closely related. Sticking to strict scientific principles, as cognitive psychologists like to do, we would need to test people in a way that time passed, but no similar events happened, and in a way that similar events happened, but no time passed. Clearly these situations are difficult to create: it is difficult to have long periods of time pass with almost no similar events occurring; and impossible to have lots of similar events occurring without time passing. Cognitive psychologists must therefore compromise with experiments that try to control each of these as best as possible.

A useful example is an ecological study that was conducted by Baddeley and Hitch (1977). The participants in their study were rugby players and they were asked to remember the names of the teams they had played against that season. Importantly, some of the players had been absent from some of the games (through injury or for other reasons). This meant that each person's experience varied according to the time since they last played (time) and the number of games they played (events). Baddeley and Hitch (1977) analysed their data and found that when it came to forgetting it wasn't time that was important but the number of intervening events. In this example, then, forgetting was due to interference – because of similar events that had occurred afterwards – or at least to a greater extent than the influence of time alone.

With the example you have just learned about, forgetting occurred because of events after the one that was forgotten. In the technical terms used in this area, this is known as 'retroactive inter- ference'. Naturally it makes some sense that if similar events occur afterwards, you may forget the specific event that you are trying to remember. It is therefore interesting to ask whether this can work the other way around: can events that happened *before* the one you are trying to remember lead to more forgetting? There is a suggestion that they can, and this is known as 'proactive inhibition' or 'proactive interference'.

A classic demonstration of proactive inhibition was provided by Underwood (1957). Like Ebbinghaus before him, he used lists of nonsense syllables as test material. Instead of testing himself, however, his participants were students from the university that he was working at. Underwood (1957) was particularly surprised to find that many of his participants were forgetting lots of the nonsense syllables a day later. Remember, you have just learned that one theory of forgetting is that similar events occurring *afterwards* cause interference, and hence forgetting. It is reasonable to assume that the participants were not going home at night and reading nonsense syllables for fun (or at least not many of them). An alternative explanation was that these parti- cipants had taken part in lots of similar experiments before (so in the past), and that this meant that they were not finding it as easy to remember these lists *now*. Underwood (1957) found out how many lists his participants might have tried to learn before (in other experiments), and was able to identify a positive relationship between rates of forgetting of these nonsense syllables and the number of lists learned previously (the more lists you have learned, the more likely you are to forget new ones). Events before the memory in question influenced forgetting, as well as the events that occurred afterwards.

Task ⎤ Try to remember the face of a classmate from school when you were very young
(maybe eight or nine years old). Ideally, try to remember the face of someone who
wasn't a close friend, and not someone you still know. Think about what makes this
task particularly difficult for some people. Is it because it was so long ago since you
last saw their face? Or is it because you have seen so many faces since? What do you
think?

The ideas of retroactive and proactive interference are only a few of the ideas that fall under
the heading of 'theories of forgetting'. It is still a continuing and exciting debate as to whether
time (trace decay), events (interference) or something else causes forgetting (see Brown and
Lewandowsky, 2010). Recent suggestions include the idea that forgetting is related to a **neuro-
biological** process labelled as 'consolidation' (e.g. Wixted, 2004) or that principles such as dis-
tinctiveness may be more important than any of these (e.g. Brown et al., 2007).

Falsely remembering

Someone I knew came from a big family of sisters, and once told me a story about her youngest
sister. The story goes that at family events this youngest sister would tell tales from her childhood
of various mishaps and scrapes that never actually happened to her, although she seemed to
strongly believe that they did (even when challenged). More often than not, they had happened
to one of the other sisters, or had simply not happened at all. No one in the family had the heart
to tell this youngest sister the truth, yet it raises an interesting question for us. How accurate is our
memory? Can something we vividly recall and clearly remember in fact be entirely false?

When someone reports something that didn't happen as if it did, psychologists refer to it as a 'false
memory'. Here we're going to discuss two different lines of research that have investigated how
vulnerable we are to this kind of thing. The first line of research focuses on a particular method
(**paradigm**) that was originally described by Deese (1959) but made more popular later on by
Roediger and McDermott (1995).

DRM paradigm

The Deese-Roediger-McDermott (DRM) paradigm (Deese, 1959; Roediger and McDermott, 1995)
is a simple, yet powerful, laboratory demonstration of our susceptibility to false remembering. In
this paradigm participants are shown lists of words and they are asked to pay attention to them
because they will need to remember them later on. These may be read out loud (auditory
presentation), shown on a computer screen or piece of paper (visual presentation), or presented
in a combination of these two methods.

Task — Below are three lists of words (don't read them yet). You will need a pen, a piece of paper and this book. When you are ready, read all three lists below at a steady pace, spending about 1 second on each word. Then shut the book and count back from 99 in threes (99, 96, 93, 90 etc.). When you reach 0, write out as many of the words that you can remember on your piece of paper. Check which words you have remembered correctly, and circle any that you wrote down but aren't on these lists. Keep reading this section of the book to learn about what may have happened.

List 1	List 2	List 3
Thread	Fast	Bed
Pin	Lethargic	Rest
Eye	Stop	Awake
Sewing	Listless	Tired
Sharp	Snail	Dream
Point	Cautious	Wake
Prick	Delay	Snooze
Thimble	Traffic	Blanket
Haystack	Turtle	Doze
Thorn	Hesitant	Slumber

Note: Lists adapted from Roediger and McDermott (1995)

The lists that are presented consist of words that are highly related to one another, for example, thread, pin, eye, sewing, sharp, point, prick. Importantly, there is always a word that is very highly associated to the words on the list but is *never* shown. This is known as a 'critical lure', and in this example the critical lure is the word 'needle'. For a list of words including fast, lethargic, stop, listless, snail, cautious, delay, the critical lure is 'slow'. The critical lure for a list containing bed, rest, awake, tired, etc. is 'sleep'.

Participants will see a small number of these lists (three or four) before being asked to demonstrate what they can remember. They may be asked simply to write down the words they can remember or to say them out loud (free recall). Alternatively, what participants can remember can be found out by showing participants a new presentation of words and asking them to indicate the ones that they think they have seen before (a recognition test). Recognition tests come in different forms, but the main idea is simple: some of the words that people are choosing from are words from the lists they have seen; some of the choices are words they haven't seen; and some of the words are the 'critical lures' (highly related words they haven't seen).

Cognitive psychologists are particularly interested in whether people indicate that they remember the critical lures (in our examples 'needle', 'slow' and 'sleep'). What Roediger and McDermott (1995) found in their first experiment was that critical lures were falsely recalled 40 per cent of the time, and were later recognised with high confidence. This first experiment was a simple replication of the early work of Deese (1959). In a second experiment, they created some new lists and were able to demonstrate a false recall rate of 55 per cent. Across these two experiments it was clearly demonstrated that, with carefully constructed lists of words, people falsely remembered highly related information that had not already been seen.

A particular strength of these findings has been that they are highly replicable: different research groups in different countries with different participants have found similar results. It has therefore been possible for many different researchers to discover new things about the different boundaries to this false memory experience. For example, we know that older adults are more susceptible to this illusion than younger adults (e.g. Norman and Schacter, 1997), and that false recall is highly related to how good you are at knowing the context of where your memories came from originally (e.g. Unsworth and Brewer, 2010).

A particular limitation of this type of research is the extent to which these findings are generalisable. It is has been suggested that interest in false memories has emerged because of an increasing number of reports of adults remembering episodes of childhood sexual abuse during therapy (e.g. Loftus, 1996). Our vulnerability to false memories, and the factors that influence them, is therefore of great interest to individuals, the legal system and researchers in general. The extent to which conclusions from such laboratory situations can be extended to traumatic childhood memories that may, or may not, have occurred is therefore very important. The extent to which the DRM paradigm can be generalised to such contexts has been questioned (Freyd and Gleaves, 1996), although some researchers have managed to link vulnerability to this paradigm with a tendency to report stories of alien abduction (Clancy et al. 2002), and memories of past lives (Meyersburg et al., 2009).

Skill builder activity

Remembering what didn't happen

Transferable skill focus: independent learning

Key question: *What influences false memories?*

It has been noted throughout this chapter that there is a large amount of research on the topics of learning and memory, and that it would be impossible to summarise it all here. The ability to do further research on your own is an important part of a skill that we call independent learning. In this chapter you have learned about a research method known as the DRM paradigm and you have learned that there has been lots of research using this paradigm since 1995. With this skill builder you have the opportunity to develop your independent learning skills through creating a 'research map' of research that uses the DRM paradigm.

An important part of being able to learn independently is finding new information to learn from. As more information becomes available online, this skill is becoming closely related to the skill of using information technology. If you did not take the opportunity to practise or develop your information technology skills using the skill builder titled 'Measuring the mind' in Chapter 1, then this may be a good opportunity to return to it. This may not be necessary if you are already confident with using information technology, such as searching the internet.

With this activity we will make use of the internet to enable you to learn independently about what has been found out using the DRM paradigm. On a computer, open up an internet browser (such as Internet Explorer, Firefox or Google Chrome) and navigate to a suitable search tool (such as www.google.co.uk or www.bing.co.uk). From here we are going to find a database of research abstracts to use. A research abstract is a short summary of a piece of research that tells you what the problem was that was being researched, what the researchers did, what they found, and what they think it means. It is possible to find databases of research abstracts that are just from psychological research. One well-known database is PsycINFO® but you may need to pay to use it. If you are currently studying at university or college, then where you are studying may already be paying for you to have access and it is worth checking with them to see if you can use it. There are currently freely available databases such as PubMED that are not specific to psychological research but are more helpful than a general search of the whole internet. If you do not have access to PsycINFO®, then use a search tool to find the website for PubMED.

Now that you are on a website that provides a database of research abstracts, use the search facility to look for 'DRM False Memory' or a similar combination of words. A (very) long list of titles of research will be displayed. You may, or may not, have to click on the title to be able to read the whole abstract depending on the database you are using. Choose a title that appeals to you, for example *Effects of cell-phone and text message distractions on true and false recognition*. This is the title of an article by Smith et al. (2011). Read the abstract and try to determine the main finding of the research. In this example the main finding was that memory for words that had been seen was lower if the participants were distracted by cell-phone and text messages, but this made no difference to their false memories (memories for words they had not seen). Make a note of this main finding on a big blank piece of paper.

Repeat this exercise for another four or five abstracts (or as many as you like). Now, when you have a look at your piece of paper you will see that you have the start of a 'map' of research findings in this area. To begin to understand the 'terrain' of this map, try to find links between the pieces of research. Are some of the findings similar? Are they the same 'place'? Are some of the findings very different? Are they different 'places'? Use arrows, notes, highlighting or whatever system you like to insert these links or differences into your map. Once you have started to make changes, you may find it useful to draw out your map again on a new piece of paper to better illustrate what you have found.

If you want to continue your independent learning, then take this map and go back to the database where you started and continue to explore. Just like an explorer in the real world, you have lots of options when considering how to proceed. You could go to a specific area of the map and explore it in more detail, perhaps using search terms from the titles of the articles that you have put in that 'place'. Alternatively, you could try to discover whole new areas of terrain, or try to find whether there are any links ('roads') between different areas. There are many possibilities and I encourage you to try many of them out and see what you learn. This potential to find out about new ideas is what makes discovery about science, through independent learning, so exciting.

Skill builder review

This activity helps develop your independent learning skills. While textbooks and lectures can provide useful 'landmarks' for the world of research, independent learning about psychological research can feel like entering an overwhelming world of data and findings, and can sometimes be difficult and intimidating to navigate. Creating, updating and revising 'research maps' can be a useful way of not only summarising what you find but guiding your independent learning activities and structuring your own thoughts about a topic.

Other skills you may have used in this activity include: information technology; organisational skills; problem solving; and decision making.

Eyewitness testimony

A particular concern for many psychologists has been whether memories can be changed after the event. That is, can a false memory be created because of post-event information such as the way that people are questioned?

Loftus and colleagues have been interested in whether the very precise wording of a question can change someone's memory for an event that they have witnessed. In a classic study, Loftus and Palmer (1974) showed their participants films of car accidents taken from safety training videos. After each film participants were asked to write down what had happened before answering a set of specific questions. Among these questions was one about the speed of the cars: *About how fast were the cars going when they hit each other?* The key word in this question was the word *hit*. Equal numbers of participants had either the word *hit* or an alternative from the following list: *smashed*; *collided*; *bumped*; and *contacted*. The researchers wanted to know if the word they used would influence the average speed estimates of the participants. Interestingly, it did. Loftus and Palmer (1974) found that participants who were asked how fast the cars were going when they *smashed* on average estimated a speed of 40.8 mph, while participants who were asked how fast the cars were going when they *contacted* each other estimated, on average, a speed of 31.8 mph.

In a second experiment, Loftus and Palmer (1974) asked their participants to watch just one film and then they were questioned in the same way. A third of participants were asked about speed when they *smashed*, a third were asked about speed when they *hit*, and a third weren't asked about speed at all. All of these participants were asked a second set of questions a week later. A key question was, *Did you see any broken glass?* Loftus and Palmer (1974) wanted to know if the type of verb had changed the memory for the participants in terms of more than just speed estimates. They found that participants who had earlier been questioned using the verb *smashed* were more likely to say that they had seen broken glass when compared to the other participants who had heard *hit* or weren't asked about speed at all. This clearly demonstrated that specific details about what people claim to remember can be influenced by the words that are used during questioning.

One alternative explanation of these results is that the participants were responding according to how they thought they should in this situation (social pressure), for example, through the desire not to appear stupid or a desire to please the experimenter. In other words, it is possible that these differences emerge because of the situation of the experiment, rather than any changes in participants' actual memories. This is also known as the **demand characteristics** of an experiment. In 1980, Loftus repeated the basic experiment but provided monetary incentives for participants to get things completely correct. Even under these conditions of high incentive, the false reporting of events continued. On the basis of this evidence it can be argued that the original findings are not the result of demand characteristics but instead represent actual false memories.

Interestingly, it has been suggested that the influence of biased instructions can extend as far as to increasing confidence when incorrectly selecting a thief's face from a line-up (e.g. Leippe et al., 2009), and that creating false video evidence can even lead some people to believe they committed acts that they never did (Nash and Wade, 2009).

Assignments

1. Compare and contrast processing approaches and structural approaches to memory. Provide an example of a memory test (real or made up) and explain how both different approaches might be used to explain any results from this test. Argue for the best explanation, using other evidence from psychological research to support it.

2. Describe two different theories of how information is forgotten. State the basic ideas behind both theories, and present evidence from psychological research to support your points.

3. Evaluate the DRM paradigm. Describe, with examples, how the paradigm works and the results that are usually found. Explain the strengths of this approach when studying false memories, and discuss any weaknesses.

Summary: what you have learned

You have learned that both memory and learning have been researched lots by cognitive psychologists. You have learned that different approaches to understanding memory can be distinguished by whether they are looking at types of memory and how they are related (structural approach) or at the processes involved in a single system (processing approach). You have learned about several examples, such as distinctions in long-term memory and levels of processing.

You have also learned that some people consider memories to be highly related to each other, through spreading patterns of activation, and that context can have an influence on how well you recall something that you have learned (the encoding specificity principle). These ideas are involved when the police set up reconstructions of crimes and use cognitive interviews.

You also know that researchers suggest that a lot of information is forgotten initially, but that anything remaining after this initial period tends to last a long time. You now know of two ideas about why things are forgotten: that forgetting is influenced by time (trace decay) and by events (interference), either in the past (proactive interference) or in the future (retroactive interference). You have also learned about a major concern for cognitive psychology – ecological validity – and how it is related to research in this area.

Finally, the phenomenon of falsely remembering has been discussed and you have learned about a powerful experimental paradigm (the DRM paradigm) that can lead people to recall, with some confidence, words that they haven't been asked to remember. You have also learned that how someone is questioned can strongly influence what they recall of an event.

Throughout this chapter you have had an opportunity to develop your reflection skills through reflecting on your own assumptions about how memory works. You have also had the opportunity to develop your independent learning skills, learning about the existence of research databases and using information from these to create a 'research map' that can help guide your learning.

Further reading

Baddeley, A (2007) *Working memory, thought and action*. Oxford: Oxford University Press.

A welcome update to the seminal work on working memory published in 1986, this has a broader coverage than its predecessor and is an essential read for anyone interested in working memory.

Baddeley, A, Eysenck, MW and Anderson, MC (2009) *Memory*. Hove: Psychology Press.

An excellent accessible book that has a broad coverage, is comprehensive, and provides a good balance between classic studies and more recent developments in the field.

Brainerd, CJ and Reyna, VF (2005) *The science of false memory*. New York: Oxford University Press.

Designed to be accessible to a wider audience than just memory researchers, this is a very good place to continue reading if you have an interest in false memory research.

Chapter 4

Language

Learning outcomes

By the end of this chapter you should:

- *be able to discuss how we recognise written and spoken words;*

- *be able to describe how we comprehend sentences;*

- *be able to evaluate speech errors and what they tell us about speech production; and*

- *be able to begin to analyse and evaluate theoretical approaches, as well as develop your skills at understanding and using data.*

Introduction

We make use of many of our cognitive abilities every day, so much so that we often forget how remarkable and fascinating they are. For many cognitive psychologists, our use and understanding of language is one of the most remarkable of these. To get started, try to think of everything you do in the day that involves language. For example, do you read newspapers? Read and reply to texts? Write e-mails? Talk to friends? Listen to family? My guess is that your answer to all of these is 'yes', and of course all of these involve using language. In general, these activities either involve recognising and comprehending language, such as reading or listening, or involve producing it yourself, for example, writing or speaking. With the sounds we make out of our mouths, or the lines we draw as letters on a page, we are putting our ideas and thoughts into the minds of others. Similarly, as we listen to sounds from other people's mouths and decipher the words they have written down, we are putting into our minds their thoughts and ideas. In many ways, language is a way that our minds communicate with each other. Now what isn't fascinating about that?

In this chapter you will learn about how language is recognised, how sentences are comprehended, and how language is produced. This is a general overview of the area, and there are several questions that we will not have the space to address. For example, psychologists have investigated how language is acquired in the first place (from when we are born or before), what happens when language does not develop normally and the relationship between language and our thoughts. If you find the following ideas about comprehension, production and context fascinating, then there is a whole world of scientific literature out there that you will also enjoy.

Task — Make a list of all of the different ways you have used language in the past four hours. For example, have you texted someone? Talked to someone? Written something down? Once you have your list, put some effort into grouping these into the smallest number of categories you can. What you produce will give you an idea about the similarities and differences between the ways we use language every day.

As you start to think about language you will realise that lots of the ways we use language fall into either the category of written language or spoken language. When we think about the recognition and comprehension of language, we will therefore need to think about how we recognise words when they are spoken and words when they are written down. We will start with some important terms to get familiar with.

Important terms

The purpose of this brief section is to define some of the most important terms you will be thinking about when learning about the cognitive psychology of language. All of these are specialist words that refer to different parts, or elements, of language. You may already be familiar with some of these terms, and you will be surprised how many of the ideas you are used to even if you didn't know the term.

- **Phonology** – what we call the sounds that are associated with language.

- **Semantics** – what we call the study of meanings (e.g. what words mean).

- **Syntactics** – the order of the words (e.g. grammar).

- **Orthography** – what we call how a word is written.

- **Morphemes** – the smallest unit in a word with meaning (e.g. 'horses' has two morphemes, 'horse' and 's', which indicates it is plural).

Now you know what is meant by some of the terms, we'll get to the really interesting stuff. We'll start with how we recognise those words that others are using to communicate their ideas.

Word recognition

The first thing to note about word recognition is that we are very good at it under normal circumstances. That is to say, we are generally accurate. You will often find that accuracy of recognition is a common measure in language research. Indeed, we assume not only that we understand each word as we encounter it, but also that we interpret how it is related to all of the words around it (Beck and Carpenter, 1986). We are also very fast at it, so much so that much of the research in this topic area uses speed as a measure and results are reported in milliseconds (1,000 milliseconds = 1 second). For example, we are sometimes able to recognise written words within 150 milliseconds (Rayner and Pollatsek, 1989). Interestingly, when participants have to press a button to show they have recognised a word in a sentence, they tend to recognise it before the end of the word has even been read out (Marslen-Wilson and Tyler, 1980).

On the whole, we are also able to cope with changes in style, such as different fonts or different regional accents – although I can think of many occasions when I've been baffled by a strong accent from Glasgow or struggled to read my own writing. Nevertheless, that we are able to do this at all when there are variations is itself interesting. For convenience, we will discuss the recognition of written words and spoken words together, as the ideas involved are very similar: people tend to be good at one if they are good at the other (Daneman and Carpenter, 1980).

To understand something about word recognition we will first look at a number of things that influence how well, or how fast, we recognise words. These are:

- word frequency;

- neighbourhood effects;

- context.

Word frequency

Word frequency refers to how often, or how frequently, we have been exposed to a word. Now this is something that is very difficult to determine on an individual basis. For example, think about how often you have either read or heard the word 'animal'. Would you be able to calculate an accurate figure? Probably not. Yet frequency has an impact on our ability to recognise words.

To study the effects of frequency, researchers have created clever measures that estimate how often people, on average, may have been exposed to certain words. For example, Kucera and Francis (1967) reviewed a sample of books, magazines and other printed materials, counting the number of times each word occurred. This measure is known as written frequency, and although the measure is only approximate, it has been shown that different word frequencies have different influences on our behaviours. For example, some researchers have measured how long people look at each word when reading (known as eye fixations). They have found that low-frequency words are looked at for longer than high-frequency words even when they have a similar number of letters (Rayner and Duffy, 1986; Staub et al., 2010), and that frequency determines the speed at which people respond when they are asked to decide if a string of letters is a word or not (Whaley, 1978). There is even some evidence that frequency effects extend beyond just single words to short phrases (Arnon and Snider, 2010), and that common words are more predictable than rare words based on what came before them (McDonald and Shillcock, 2003).

Task — Choose an article from a newspaper or magazine and count the number of times each different word is used. Look at your results, and think about whether this represents how many times these words are used generally. Then choose another article in a different newspaper or article and repeat the exercise. Are the words similar or different? Why might this be?

At the start of this section we noted how hard it is to measure the number of times each individual person has been exposed to every possible word in their lifetime. Instead, researchers have had to rely on *estimates* of frequency through collecting information such as written frequency (how often a word is written in a sample of documents). This is what we would call an operational definition of the idea. The idea, or concept, is how often someone has been exposed to a word. We can't get at this exact number, but in practice we can come up with a suitable version, in this case counting the average occurrences from a range of writing. The operational definition is how we put a concept into practice in an experiment or scientific study. Psychology relies on operational definitions much more than many other sciences simply because the things we are interested in (attention, memory, perception etc.) are very difficult to measure directly. It is therefore important that we think critically about these definitions, and make sure we are happy with the way the idea has been operationalised.

Some limitations to the operational definition of word frequency have been identified. One limitation is that there are differences between how often a word is spoken (spoken frequency) and how often it is written (written frequency). For example, the personal pronoun of 'I' is ten times more common in terms of estimates of spoken frequency than those of written frequency (Dahl, 1979). Another limitation is that the frequency of words is also related to the age at which the words were first learned. This is known as age-of-acquisition, and it can also influence how quickly people perform word recognition tasks (e.g. Carroll and White, 1973). Researchers therefore have to be careful that anything they think is a frequency effect isn't actually due to how early the words were acquired by the participants. We will not be able to go into this level of detail for every measure mentioned in this book. However, always keep thinking about whether the operational definition of the concept measures what it claims to be measuring, or if it could also be measuring something else.

Importantly, these effects of word frequency are so reliable and so robust that it is essential that any explanations of word recognition are able to account for them.

Neighbourhood effects

The term 'neighbourhood effect' refers to an interesting idea about the number of 'neighbours' a word has (Coltheart et al., 1977). Let's take the example of an orthographical neighbourhood. Orthography is how a word looks, so an orthographical neighbourhood of a word means the number of other words that look like it. The way a cognitive psychologist would put this into practice is by counting the number of words that have the same length, and have the same letters except for one. For example, the word 'river' has ten orthographical neighbours, which include diver, liver, rover, rider and rivet. This is another example of an operational definition. These ideas have recently been developed to measure neighbourhood size, which includes words of different lengths as well as those of the same length. This new measure is an even stronger predictor of several different behaviours (Yarkoni et al., 2008).

Task —— Choose a four-letter word. Try to write down as many different words as you can that are also four letters long and contain at least three of the same letters in the same order. The number you get is your approximation of that word's orthographic neighbourhood.

In experiments, you find that participants respond faster to words that have lots of neighbours than to those with not so many. However, it is worth noting that this only applies to low-frequency words (e.g. Andrews 1989, 1992). Neighbourhoods can also be defined for more features than just a word's orthography. Effects have also been found for properties such as phonology (sounds of words); in recognition tasks participants have been shown to be faster at recognising words that have a larger number of phonological neighbours (e.g. Yates et al., 2004).

Context

The importance of context is something you will learn about in many of the chapters in this book. In terms of word recognition, we may be interested in whether words are recognised differently when presented in a context that makes sense. For example, Marslen-Wilson and Tyler (1980) originally found that words were recognised faster when they made sense in the context, compared to when they did not make sense. Interestingly, context doesn't appear to affect how accurate someone is in recognising a word. If a word doesn't make sense in its context, we still recognise what word it is. Instead, context influences the speed at which this process occurs (Marslen-Wilson, 1987).

Researchers also measure where people look when reading and how long for, known as eye fixation. This is another useful way of getting a measure of the processes going on in the mind when it comes to word recognition. In terms of context, it has been found that the plausibility of a word in its context can also influence how long participants spend on looking at the word for the first time (e.g. Staub et al., 2007; Warren and McConnell, 2007).

Explaining word recognition

It is nice to know about different things that influence word recognition, but what does it mean in terms of how our minds work? You have learned before that an important part of critical thinking in cognitive psychology is to question what the explanation is, on top of the results that have been described. The explanations that have been offered for word recognition rely upon a number of different ideas. One of the most important ideas is that of the **mental lexicon**.

It has been suggested that we have in our minds a store that contains information about words. For example, this store contains information about how the word is pronounced, how it is spelt and what it means. This is called a mental lexicon, and you may find it easier to think of this lexicon as a kind of mental dictionary. When we recognise a word, we are accessing this word from the mental lexicon; this is also called lexical access. Researchers differ according to whether they think words are looked up in this lexicon directly or through a more systematic search. To understand why this is important it is useful to look at the development of these models from the 1970s.

Serial search models

Looking up words as part of a systematic search is what is known as a serial search model of lexical access (e.g. Forster, 1976). In this sort of model the lexicon contains a master file of words. Each file is linked to a series of 'access files', in the same way that a webpage might have a number of relevant terms that come up in an online search. In this model there are orthographic access files, phonological access files and semantic/syntactic access files. When someone perceives a word, a search is carried out through the access files until a match is found. This access file then gives directions to the master file, like a link in an online search, and this master file has all the information about the word, such as its meaning. To make the process better, the access files are organised in 'bins' according to properties such as the sound of the first letter or the word frequency.

The logogen model

An alternative to the idea of serial search is the idea that words are accessed directly. An important version of this idea is the logogen model (Morton 1969, 1970). This model makes use of the idea of **thresholds** and **activation**. If you're not sure what a threshold is, imagine it like a wall. For something to get over the wall it requires energy, which we'll call activation. Various things contribute to activation until there is enough to pass the threshold to be recognised. In our analogy, this is like getting enough energy to get over the wall.

The logogen model suggests that each word in the lexicon is represented by a 'logogen'. This logogen passively counts the features of a word that is being said or read, and this changes their level of activation. For example, if the phoneme /ch/ is detected, then all of the logogens with this phoneme will be partially activated; this may include the logogens for *church*, *chair* and *charity*. If the word is part of a conversation about buying furniture, then the logogen for *chair* will receive a little more activation, as well as partially activating logogens for other types of furniture such as *bed* and *wardrobe*. Once a logogen has enough activation, it will be recognised as the correct word and all of its lexical entry will be used in the processes that follow.

Task — In your own words, summarise the main differences between a serial search approach to lexical access and the logogen model. Use examples to illustrate your ideas.

These ideas of activation and thresholds continue in current models of word recognition. In particular, they are an important part of what are known as **connectionist** models of word recognition (e.g. Seidenberg and McClelland, 1989; Plaut et al., 1996). These models are too complicated to explain here, and might need a whole chapter to themselves, but it is important to know that they exist and that they make use of different layers of features (such as orthography and phonology) that are all interconnected and rely on activation levels and associations between them. These models make use of a lot of computations, and are far from straightforward, but they have been shown to be able to behave in similar ways to human participants.

The cohort model

If we turn our attention to spoken word recognition, then similar ideas emerge in what is known as the cohort model (e.g. Marslen-Wilson and Welsh, 1978; Marslen-Wilson, 1987, 1990). Like the logogen model, each word has its own representation in the lexicon. In this model they are known as units or nodes rather than logogens. According to this model, a listener does not wait until a whole word has been heard before identifying it. Instead, after the first few phonemes, the options from all possible words are narrowed down to all of those that contain these phonemes. This 'narrowing down' occurs as words are activated (that is, they receive some sort of mental energy), and that creates a set of words beginning with these sounds. This is known as the word initial cohort. Words that are activated more frequently (heard more often) become more active at this stage. As more phonemes are perceived, the activation levels of non-relevant words decline, until one word is left with high activation levels. The context of any sentence is also used to eliminate words that wouldn't make sense. The uniqueness point is the point in the process where there is only a single word left. This can therefore happen before the end of the word being said, which may explain why some words are recognised before the person you're listening to has finished saying them (O'Rourke and Holcomb, 2002).

Like the logogen model described above, the cohort model involves lots of parts of the lexicon being activated in parallel. Unlike the logogen model, this explanation does not rely upon a threshold being reached; instead, it makes use of a process in which possible alternatives are eliminated. The models therefore differ in terms of the specific processes that take place.

In this section you have learned about a small number of ideas about how we access representations of words in our mental lexicon. This is only one aspect of what is a complicated task. Once the representations are accessed, we need to think about how this information is actually stored in the lexicon and what that means for our processing. We need to think about the visual aspects of the processing – what it means to see the lips moving on someone's face and how this influences speech recognition. We also need to think about how we break up speech so that we understand it as separate words and about what it means to read a word rather than hear one, and the processes necessary to understand reading. All of these aspects are beyond the scope of this short chapter, but I strongly recommend you use the suggested further readings to learn more if you're interested. One important aspect that we *will* consider is how we begin to comprehend these individual words as a whole sentence with meaning.

Sentence comprehension

While working out how words are recognised poses challenges, we must remember that this is an important part of understanding the message that is being communicated. Apart from very simple utterances (such as 'Quick!'), words are generally part of more meaningful sentences. You have already learned that words are recognised before people get to the end of them, and the same is also true of whole sentences. An important part of the process of sentence comprehension is, therefore, how syntax is processed.

Syntactic structures

Syntax refers to the rules that govern how words are put together to form sentences. You may already know of the most common forms of syntax from your experiences at school – what we might call grammar. Grammar will have a big impact on the meaning of a sentence. For example, consider the following sentence:

Caroline jumped on Matthew

This sentence has a subject, an object and a verb (you may remember some of this from English lessons at school). The subject is Caroline, and the object is Matthew. These are both nouns, and in between them you will usually find a verb (an action word). The verb here is the action of jumping on. This word order is often indicated as SVO because it goes in the order Subject, Verb and then Object. We can easily change the meaning of the sentence by moving the nouns around. Consider this revised sentence:

Matthew jumped on Caroline

The meaning of the sentence has now changed, and the idea processed by your mind will be different. Matthew has become the subject, Caroline becomes the object, and it is Matthew who is doing the 'jumping on' to Caroline. Note that by simply moving the nouns we have altered the meaning of the sentence; this is because our syntax (rules of grammar) tell, us that the noun that comes first is the subject, and the noun that comes last is the object. Both sentences still have an SVO construction; the meaning changed when we moved the words around (rather than the rules of grammar changing).

One estimate suggests that 75 per cent of languages use this SVO construction (Ratner and Gleason, 1993). Exceptions include Japanese, which uses SOV (Caroline Matthew jumped on), and Welsh, which uses VSO (jumped on Caroline Matthew).

In cognitive models of sentence comprehension, the process of working out the structure of a sentence is known as parsing. It is suggested that there are a number of different clues and strategies that we use to do this.

Parsing sentences

Like the recognition of words, we know that sentences are also comprehended before they are finished. This suggests that the process of parsing is something that happens as the sentence continues rather than after the end of that part of the sentence. Researchers have found that when participants encounter words that could be either a noun or a verb in an incomplete sentence, they will use the information that came before it to decide which it is (Tyler and Marslen-Wilson, 1977). This type of processing is known as incremental processing, because it occurs in steps as the sentence is experienced or perceived.

In an attempt to specify these processes more exactly, Frazier (1979) suggested that each word is assigned a syntactic role in the sentence as it is encountered. Importantly, it was argued that in cases where this is unclear (i.e. it could be a noun or a verb) a reader or listener will make a decision rather than wait to see or hear the rest of the sentence. By making this decision as the sentence progresses, we can make mistakes. You may have heard the phrase 'being led down the garden path'. This notion that people may go down the wrong path because they made a wrong decision early on is actually used for this model of parsing – it is known as the garden path model. Research in this specific area therefore uses 'garden path' sentences. These are sentences that people may struggle to understand correctly the first time they read them because they get misled. An often-quoted example is the following from Bever (1970):

The horse raced past the barn fell.

In reading this sentence you may have wanted to insert extra words so it made sense to you. For example, you may have wanted to change it to *The horse that raced past the barn fell*, maybe *The horse raced past the barn and fell* or even *The horse raced past, and the barn fell*. For psychologists this is very interesting, and we can use it to investigate some of the processes that are going on.

Task — Create two new examples of a 'garden path' sentence such as the example given above. It is not as easy as it sounds. Show them to a friend or member of your family and ask them to read them out loud. Notice if they get stuck and repeat any of the words, maybe to change the way they are saying it or the meaning they are attaching to the words.

Frazier (1979) proposed a number of rules that we might use to determine which potential version of the sentence we tend to accept when we first encounter it. While there isn't space for you to learn about all of these here, it is important to learn that this idea relies upon us only having one mental version of the sentence at any point in time and on each word's role in that sentence being based on syntactic features. What this means is that things such as the context of the sentence are not taken into account. This is important because research has shown that garden path effects can be either reduced or eliminated when the misleading interpretation isn't particularly plausible (Trueswell et al., 1994). This is referred to as semantic plausibility and is a difficult problem for any approach to parsing that suggests that only syntactic information is used.

An alternative view would be one in which multiple possible versions of a sentence are kept in mind, with different versions being eliminated when they don't make sense. Models of parsing that adopt this approach are known as constraint-based models (e.g. MacDonald et al., 1994). Interestingly, these models not only consider syntax but also make use of information such as how often certain syntactic structures occur (Trueswell, 1996).

Some of the constraints within these models can include structural aspects of the sounds we hear. If a sentence is spoken by someone else, then we can use how they say it to try to help parse the sentence out. For example, nouns are almost always stressed on the first syllable, whereas verbs are more likely to have the emphasis placed on the second syllable (Kelly and Bock, 1988). Try saying the word 'watch' in terms of it being something you tell the time with or as an instruction to look at something. In theory you will end up stressing the /ch/ sound more when you are using it as a verb (to watch). Similarly, we know that people make use of different aspects of pitch and timing (Warren, 1996) as well as context, influencing sentence processing at an early stage (e.g. Tanenhaus et al., 1995).

Critical thinking activity

Parsing trends

Critical thinking focus: analysing and evaluating

Key question: *Which is the best approach to understanding how we parse sentences: a serial approach or a parallel approach?*

If you completed the critical thinking activity in Chapter 2 (pages 23–4), then you will already be familiar with the following task. In the activity in Chapter 2 we focused upon analytical criteria such as: the strength of the evidence; the precision of the theory; and the ease of interpretation. In this activity we will practise using a few more criteria while evaluating two potential approaches to sentence parsing.

To help you to do this, draw a large table with the following details. In the far left column put the heading 'theoretical approach', and underneath this two rows labelled 'serial approach' and 'parallel approach'. Use the columns of the table to make notes about these approaches against a number of criteria. The following criteria need one column each.

- Similarities. (Document any similarities between the approaches. What ideas are the same across both?)

- Differences. (Note down any key aspects of the approaches that are different. What does one approach assume that the other one doesn't?)

- Generality. (Decide how much each approach can account for all the phenomena. Does one approach account for a greater number of phenomena than the other?)

- Overall. (Give an overall analysis of the approach based on your answers in the previous columns.)

Complete the table using the information you have here. Once you have completed the table you should not only have an overall evaluation but also some reasoning as to why you have reached these conclusions. If you feel adventurous, read other textbooks or journal articles to see if you can fill out more information in each column. You may find that this changes your overall analysis.

Critical thinking review

This activity helps develop your analysis and evaluation skills in relation to how we parse sentences in language comprehension. You were encouraged to use a specific set of criteria (similarities, differences and generality). These criteria are only a few of those that people have used to analyse and evaluate theoretical approaches. You may also think about: whether the approach is precisely defined; if it does more than describe what is known; and if it is easy to make new and novel predictions using it.

Being able to analyse and evaluate information in this way is an important skill to develop as you learn how to make your own judgements about ideas and theories. In the 'real world' such skills are crucial in making sense of the world in an informed and intelligent way, not just in your academic study.

Other skills you may have used in this activity include: reflection; critical thinking; decision making; independent learning; and problem solving.

You may also be interested to learn that parsing of sentences is completed more efficiently with more experience (e.g. Reali and Christiansen, 2007). Interestingly, an alternative approach to the ones you have learned about is to process sentences to a level that is 'good enough' for whatever task you're doing (e.g. Swets et al., 2008). This is particularly important because it challenges the assumption that the aim is to process a sentence in a detailed and accurate way. This assumption underpins the approaches highlighted here, but it is entirely possible that sentences are processed in a detailed way only when it is necessary for what the person is doing.

In this section you have briefly learned about two different models of how parsing occurs, to help us comprehend sentences. It is important to note that a number of other explanations exist that are worthy of your attention if you are interested. Very recently, some researchers have even claimed to have modelled sentence parsing using simulations of neurons in the brain (e.g. Huyck, 2009). For now, we will leave recognition and comprehension behind and instead focus upon actually producing speech to communicate your own ideas back.

Speech production

As you learn about speech production in this section you will probably notice that, in comparison to recognition and comprehension, we know relatively little about the cognitive psychology of it. The methods we have available to us are part of the reason for this. You have already learned that an important aspect of cognitive psychology is that we are studying the mind in a scientific way. Using a scientific method means that we are very careful about controlling what happens in an experiment so that we can conclude that the thing that is changing our measure (our dependent variable) is what we've manipulated (our independent variable). The level of control that we need is relatively easy when we study recognition and comprehension because the researcher is in control of the words that are seen or heard, and it is just the task of the participant to respond to them. If you think about it briefly, you will realise that studying how a participant produces speech is a lot harder, and it is much more difficult to do it in the controlled and scientific way that we would like. Simply telling people what to say is not ideal because it removes lots of the natural aspects of the speech process. One approach that has been adopted is to study the errors that people make, in the hope that these errors will reveal something about the processes that underlie them.

Speech errors

A speech error is when you say something that you did not intend, or make a mistake when you are talking to someone. You may also know them as 'slips of the tongue'. These mistakes are potentially revealing because they may tell us something about the processes of speech production that resulted in the error.

In the late 1960s and early 1970s researchers collected detailed records of the types of errors that people made (Fromkin, 1971; Garrett, 1975). When these errors were analysed it became clear that they weren't random. Instead, there were systematic patterns within them. Garrett (1975, 1984) highlighted four types of speech errors in particular. You will now learn about each of these in turn.

Word exchanges

A word exchange is when words from the same category swap position in the sentence. In other words, two nouns will change places, or two adjectives will change places. Here are two examples.

I'm sending a friend to my text < I'm sending a text to my friend

That rubbish is car < That car is rubbish

Sound exchanges

A sound exchange is similar to a word exchange except it is not the whole word that is in the wrong place but just a sound within it. Interestingly, this mainly occurs with words that are next to each other in the sentence. Here are two more examples.

I saw an endian iliphant at the zoo < I saw an Indian elephant at the zoo

How big is snhat thail? < How big is that snail?

Morpheme exchanges

You have already learned that a morpheme is the smallest unit of meaning that a word can be divided into. You can have 'root morphemes' which are the core of a word (such as *run* or *write*), or the inflectional morphemes you'd find at the end of a word (such as *-ing* or *–s*). A morpheme exchange is when part of the word gets 'stranded' and attached to a new one. Here are examples.

She texts her hating < She hates her texting

He rags her runned < He runs her ragged

Word substitutions

Unlike an exchange, a word substitution is an error when a different word is substituted for the one that was intended. Interestingly, this happens only with content words and certain prepositions. Again, here are examples.

Let's go to the shop when it's closed < Let's go to the shop when it's open

Pass me the pepper < Pass me the salt

Serial models of speech production

As interesting as these errors are, we need to think about what sort of language production processes would result in us making such mistakes. One proposition was a model put forward by Garrett (1975, 1984). This model is illustrated in Figure 4.1.

To understand this model you will have to learn a little about what happens at each level. The message level consists of the basic ideas that the speaker intends to communicate to listeners. This then proceeds to the functional level where these ideas are linked to meaningful representations in the mental lexicon (the mental dictionary). The words are assigned roles in the syntax (e.g. subject, object, verb), but the order of the words is not yet decided upon. Then, at the positional level, the words are put in a specific order in the developing sentence. This then proceeds to the phonetic level where very specific information about how the words are pronounced is included, before proceeding to the articulation level, which contains very specific commands for how the sentence will be physically produced by your lips and your tongue.

Figure 4.1: *A model of speech production as proposed by Garrett (1984)*

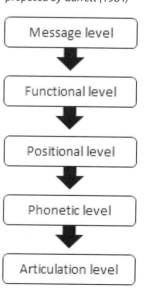

Let's apply this to an example of the errors that you learned about earlier. An important aspect of the above model is that the grammatical roles are decided at the functional level, and the appropriate words to fit into that structure are then chosen at the positional level. This would explain why we get word exchanges where a noun at the start of a sentence and a noun at the end of a sentence might get mixed up (e.g. I'm sending a friend to my text) and yet the correct grammatical structure is kept. The grammatical structure is defined earlier in the process (at an earlier level), and the nouns are put in at a later level, so they still make grammatical sense despite the error. Interpreting speech errors using this model therefore involves thinking carefully about which level the error occurs at and what is 'in place' before the mistake is made.

Task — In your own words, summarise the main stages of Garrett's (1975, 1984) model of speech production. Try to include examples to illustrate your thoughts whenever you can.

An important aspect to notice is that the model proposes that production happens in a series of stages, each completed in a specific order. This is known as a **serial model** of speech production because of this. Similar serial models have been proposed by other researchers (e.g. Levelt, 1989; Levelt et al., 1999), and if you are interested in this type of model, I recommend you do some further reading about these.

You have already learned in this chapter that an alternative to serial processes is a model in which processes happen at roughly the same time. These are known as **parallel models**, or interactive models, and they are as important to think about with speech production as they are with language recognition. For example, Dell (1986; Dell and O'Seagdha, 1992) has proposed a model of speech production in which the different levels of speech (e.g. semantics, phonology) are processed in parallel in an interactive way. Just like the connectionist models we learned about briefly in terms of word recognition, a full explanation of this model would require a lot more space and detail than we have available to us. However, it is important to know that these exist.

Skill builder activity

I'm not drunk but I may be a tittle lipsy

Transferable skill focus: understanding and using data

Key question: *What type of speech errors do people make?*

You have learned that one way to study speech production is to look at the errors that people make. Garrett (1975, 1984) documented around 3,400 of these speech errors occurring in natural speech. In this activity you will do the same, but on a much smaller scale.

Just collecting these errors is not enough in itself. Garrett then had to analyse them to work out how the errors could be grouped together. You have learned about four of these groupings: word exchanges; sound exchanges; morpheme exchanges; and word substitutions. There are also a few more you have not learned about yet. To complete this activity you might find it useful to remind yourself about these types of error.

Once these groupings were established Garrett (1984) interpreted them in terms of a model of speech production. This stage is very important because, as cognitive psychologists, we must be able to suggest what something means in terms of processes in the mind. It is not enough to redescribe what our results are, even if they are very interesting on their own. If results are re-presented in different terms but no explanation is added, we would say they were too descriptive and not explanatory. When thinking critically about models and theories, this is an important thing to watch out for.

This activity requires you to create your own (smaller) collection of speech errors. The aim is for you to have a list of at least 20 different speech errors. When you hear someone make a mistake in what they are saying, make a note of it in a notebook, a diary or a document on your computer. Make sure you keep a record of what they meant to say, as well as what was said. This may take some time to build up, but it is very interesting and you'll be surprised just how many errors people make when you're keeping records of them. If you want to speed the process up a little, you can always look at collections of 'bloopers' or 'out-takes' from your favourite TV shows. These are sometimes provided as additional features on DVDs or Blu-rays, or you can find them on some internet sites (e.g. YouTube). However, remember that you need to know what was meant to be said. In addition, these errors are less natural and are not as useful as real errors made in unscripted situations.

Once you have your collection of speech errors, you will need to try to group them into similar errors. Have a look at what has happened. Have sounds moved around? Or whole words? Did they use a word they didn't mean to use? See how many of the errors fit into those groupings you have learned about already: word exchanges; sound exchanges; morpheme exchanges; and word substitutions. In addition, have a close look at all of those speech errors that don't fit into these categories. Come up with a short 100-word description of the type of error being made for any additional groupings you find.

Finally, you'll need to become familiar again with the model proposed by Garrett (1984). If you cannot remember it, then look back at Figure 4.1. For each grouping you have identified, including those you knew about already, try to write down 150 words on why these errors happen in terms of this model. Importantly, use the examples for the unique data that you have collected to explain the ideas.

Skill builder review

This activity helps develop your skills at understanding and using data. While reading about examples of speech errors can be entertaining, it is important to remember that our aim as cognitive psychologists is to explain the processing of information in the human mind. Interpreting and using data is an important part of this, and you have begun to develop invaluable experience as part of this skill builder activity. Importantly, it should have not been particularly easy. Understanding and using data is challenging, and it is important to learn that while these analyses may seem straightforward when written about in textbooks, they can be a lot more difficult than you'd expect. Practice and experience are very important in developing these skills.

Other skills you may have used in this activity include: independent learning; decision making; organisational skills; and problem solving.

Beyond waiting for speech errors

It was noted at the beginning of this section on speech production that it is difficult to investigate production using experiments. You have therefore learned about models of naturally occurring speech errors, and one way of thinking about speech production that might help explain these. The final part of this chapter will look at one example of how some researchers have tried to go beyond waiting for speech errors to occur naturally.

One approach to studying speech production in an experimental way has involved trying to induce speech errors through giving participants a particularly difficult task. Levelt et al. (1991) asked their participants to take part in an experiment where they would have to produce speech and complete a word recognition test at the same time. The speech production part of the task required participants to name pictures as quickly as possible. The word recognition part of the task involved them listening to a spoken word through some headphones and pressing a button as soon as they recognised it. Some of the words they heard were completely unrelated to the picture being viewed. Some of the words were related to the picture by their meaning (semantics), while some of the words were related to the picture by their sounds (phonology). Finally, some of the words were related to the picture through links created by both the sounds and the meaning (phonology and semantics). One of the main measures they looked at was whether recognising a related word helped the participant name the picture faster compared to recognising an unrelated word.

It was found that semantically related words helped with the naming task, but only after very short delays such as 100ms. Phonologically related words helped with the naming task, but only after a longer delay such as 600ms. The related words that had two links (phonology and semantics) did not help at all. These results were therefore interpreted as supporting a serial model of speech production in which the different aspects, such as semantics and phonology, have differing levels of importance at different stages.

Assignments

1. Compare and contrast the logogen model of word recognition and the cohort model of spoken word recognition. Describe the basic principles of both models. Use examples to illustrate the similarities and differences between these approaches.

2. Evaluate the idea that sentence parsing occurs in an incremental way. Describe, with example sentences, an incremental model of parsing. Explain the strengths of this approach when accounting for sentence comprehension, and discuss any limitations.

3. Describe two types of speech error and explain what they might tell us about speech production. State the basic ideas behind both errors, create examples to illustrate your thoughts, and use an appropriate theory to explain why they might occur.

Summary: what you have learned

This chapter has investigated the curious case of human language use, in which we use words and sentences to communicate ideas between our minds.

You have learned that we often recognise words before we've heard them, or read them, in their entirety. You now know that word recognition is influenced by things such as word frequency, word neighbourhoods and context. You also know about three important approaches to trying to explain word recognition: serial search; the logogen model; and the cohort model.

You have learned that comprehending sentences makes use of particular grammatical structures. You now know that the process of understanding a sentence involves parsing and that this process may be completed in a sequential way or potentially through parallel processes. You have also learned that parsing can make use of additional clues in speech, such as tone and intonation.

Finally, you have learned that producing speech is a difficult topic to study in a scientific way. You now know that researchers have tended towards naturally occurring speech errors such as word exchanges, sound exchanges, morpheme exchanges and word substitutions. You are now aware of one model that may explain these errors that relies upon speech being produced in a sequential way.

Throughout this chapter you have had opportunities to develop your analytical and evaluation skills, particularly through comparing serial and parallel models of sentence parsing. You have also had the opportunity to develop your experience of understanding and using data through your own small-scale study of speech errors.

Further reading

Harley, TA (2009) *Talking the talk*. Hove: Psychology Press.

An introductory look at how humans use language that is aimed at individuals with little or no background in this area, presented in a clear and accessible way.

Harley, TA (2012) *The psychology of language: from data to theory*. 4th edition. Hove: Psychology Press

An update to an excellent text, this is a much more comprehensive look at the subject area, ideal for the confident reader who wants to learn more.

Saxton, M (2010) *Child language: acquisition and development*. London: Sage.

Clear and accessible, this book is ideal if you wish to learn how children acquire their first language, a topic that is important to the psychology of language that has not been covered here.

Chapter 5

Perception

Learning outcomes

By the end of this chapter you should:

- *be able to describe principles of perceptual organisation;*

- *be able to identify perceptual constancies and visual illusions;*

- *be able to discuss how patterns and objects may be recognised;*

- *be able to analyse different approaches to understanding visual perception; and*

- *be able to think critically and creatively about psychological phenomena, as well as developing your visual communication skills.*

Introduction

How do we see? How do we taste? How do we smell? How do we feel? And how do we hear? We've already defined cognitive psychology as the scientific study of the mind, so you may be wondering why I am asking these questions in the first place. The answer is simple: while the answers depend upon the biological structure of our sense organs (such as our eyes, ears, nose, tongue and skin), they also depend upon how the information provided by these sense organs is processed by our mind.

We will focus upon how our minds process information to give us our experience of perception. For the purposes of the chapter you will learn about perception from visual experience more than from other forms. We will do this because more is known about visual perception – as a research area it has received more attention, and for a longer period of time. More importantly, when learning about something from a book it is much easier to demonstrate visual principles than those based on, say, touch or smell, and being able to experience demonstrations is an important part of learning about perception. In keeping with other chapters, our brief coverage will give you only an introductory understanding of what is a fascinating and wide-ranging field. However, I hope that finding out some answers to the following questions will prove both enlightening and interesting.

- How does the mind organise what we see?

- What can illusions teach us about the mind?

- How do we recognise things as objects or patterns?

- Do our minds influence perception or is it just the environment?

Overall we will be looking at how our minds process information to give us the visual experience we have every day.

Perceptual organisation

Our first stop is the idea that our minds allow us to see our visual world in an organised way. That we see the world in an organised way is something we take for granted. Stop to think about it and you'll realise that it is an astonishing ability. Let's demonstrate this with a simple thought experiment. Imagine you are sitting at a table watching a friend or relative move around a room doing something – it can be anything. Now remember that the light from them is hitting the back of your eye (your retina) as a two-dimensional image. Imagine them moving around the room and think of the changes in that pattern on your retina. For a start, imagine that the person walks towards you. The pattern of them on your retina will get larger – do you think they are growing? The person then walks further away again, and the image of them gets smaller – do you think they are shrinking? They stand behind a table – do you think they are a floating torso? If they turn sideways, do you think their shape has changed? Do you still recognise them? Why am I asking stupid questions? Well, if you think about it, these aren't actually stupid questions. With the little information that is on those images on your retina these could all be possibilities. Something on the image getting bigger could mean that the thing is getting bigger (not closer). That we don't have these false beliefs is down to the power and influence of our minds.

How these basic sensations get organised is where we'll start this journey, and we'll begin at the roots of an early attempt to understand how our minds organise the world: *Gestalt* laws of organisation.

Gestalt laws

The term *Gestalt* is associated with a group of German psychologists and researchers who published most of their work at the start of the twentieth century. *Gestalt* indicates a particular approach to psychology that argues that humans deal with things as 'wholes' rather than individual parts. *Gestalt* psychology is heavily associated with the phrase 'the whole is different from the sum of its parts', a principle that was applied a lot when Max Wertheimer, a famous *Gestalt* psychologist, began to publish his findings on how the mind organises the individual parts of a scene. Using simple line drawings, he demonstrated a number of important principles that continue to remain influential (for a short review of this influence, see Rock and Palmer, 1990). Our next demonstrations are therefore five of these *Gestalt* laws of organisation. Each of the figures is adapted from the original illustrations by Wertheimer (1923).

In Figure 5.1 you will see a set of eight circles that don't appear to be grouped or organised in any particular way other than in a straight line. This is a very simple display and is one that we will refer back to as we progress.

Figure 5.1:
A demonstration of no particular perceptual grouping

The *Gestalt* law of proximity is demonstrated in Figure 5.2. Elements that are close together are seen to group together, so in this figure you are likely to perceive four groups with two dots each (compare this to Figure 5.1) rather than just a straight line of dots.

Figure 5.2:
A demonstration of perceptual grouping by proximity

If dots are equal distances apart but share something that makes them similar, they are also perceived as grouping together. This is known as the principle of similarity and is illustrated in Figure 5.3, in which you are likely again to perceive four groups with two dots each (but for different reasons).

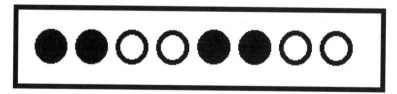

Figure 5.3:
A demonstration of perceptual grouping by similarity

Figure 5.4 illustrates the principle of closure: that we fill in the gaps to see a complete or whole object. In this demonstration you will most likely perceive four objects rather than eight separate shapes.

Figure 5.4:
A demonstration of perceptual grouping by closure

Finally, Wertheimer (1923) also observed that we see things according to the version that produces the smoothest possible lines with no breaks in continuation. This is known as the principle of good continuation and is illustrated in Figure 5.5, in which we see two smooth lines that cross over each other, rather than two 'V' shapes that are touching at their points.

Figure 5.5:
A demonstration of good continuation

A further principle has been proposed by Palmer (1992), that of common region. The principle states that we tend to group elements together that are considered to be in the same common region. In Figure 5.6 this is illustrated through additional borders that define four common regions, again leading us to perceive this as four separate groups of two dots.

Figure 5.6:
A demonstration of perceptual grouping by common region (adapted from Palmer, 1992)

Task — In your own words, describe three of the *Gestalt* laws of perceptual organisation. Try to generate different diagrams to illustrate the same principle.

Importantly, these principles have remained unchallenged throughout the years and have even been used to study the effectiveness of webpage designs (Hsiao and Chou, 2006) as well as more generally in art and design (e.g. Behrens, 2002), linguistics (e.g. Croft and Cruse, 2004) and other disciplines. The principles have remained unchallenged for a number of important reasons that are interesting to understand if you want to become a critical thinker about psychology.

When evaluating an approach in psychology it is important to think about, among other things, whether it is descriptive and how broadly the findings can be applied. When we consider if an approach is descriptive, we ask ourselves *Does it do more than describe the findings?* Theories that are more than descriptive have some sort of **predictive power** (they can be used to predict new findings). A prominent criticism of the *Gestalt* laws of organisation is that they are only descriptive. They describe the experience, but they are difficult to make new and novel predictions with. This may be a little clearer if we also think about the second point of evaluation: whether the results can be applied widely.

A difficulty with these principles for many psychologists is the idea that they cannot be easily applied to situations other than two-dimensional displays (books, websites, paintings etc.). Ideally, any account of perceptual organisation should be applicable to the three-dimensional world that we live in.

The enduring nature of the *Gestalt* account has in part been due to the lack of a better alternative for how we organise our visual worlds. Instead, researchers have focused on a number of different aspects of how our minds interpret our visual experiences in terms of more real-life scenarios where we move around, and things move around with us.

Constancies and illusions

You have learned that a limitation to *Gestalt* laws of organisation is that the situation is far more complicated if we try to apply them to real objects in three-dimensional space. Determining where things are in terms of the three-dimensional world that we live in requires our mind to use information that we know about the environment to interpret the images on the retina of our eyes. A number of rules have been identified that help us to do this. We refer to these as constancies because they are properties of the environment that do not change. For example, we know that the size of an object stays constant (things rarely change drastically in size), so something far away will appear smaller than something nearby, although we know that it is not actually smaller (it is just further away). This is known as size constancy. We also know that shape stays constant, so if a door opens, you know that it keeps its shape even though the image on the retina will change. Similarly, if a car turns a corner you know that it is not changing its shape as it moves, although the shape on the retina is, of course, changing. This is known as shape constancy.

We also know how things interact with distance. So we know that if one object obscures another, then the first one is closer to us; if we know the size of an object, we can use the image on our retina to estimate how far away it is; we know that objects that are far away are less distinct than those nearby; and that objects further away generally appear higher up in our visual fields. All of these constancies from the environment and our experience mean that we are able to judge, fairly accurately, where objects are positioned in space.

Task ⌐ Draw a picture that illustrates two of the constancies of perception. Clearly label up how each of these constancies is applied when viewing the picture.

On the one hand, these constancies are interesting because they help us get a more accurate perception of the world. We know our friend is in the distance and getting closer, rather than incredibly small, floating and rapidly increasing in size (the rule of size constancy). Yet these aspects of our visual system can also trick our minds with what are called visual illusions. If you search for them you will be able to find many different visual illusions. Below we will discuss a few of these.

In Figure 5.7 you will see two lines with arrows at the ends. Your task is to judge which of the middle lines is the longest. Have you made a decision? Well, the accepted wisdom is that most people would judge the top line (with the arrows pointing in) as being the longest. This is known as the Müller-Lyer illusion (Müller-Lyer, 1889), and it is an illusion because both of the lines are the same length. If you don't believe me, use bits of paper, or something else, to cover the arrows and check. The exact explanation for this illusion is still a matter for debate, but one explanation was provided by Gregory (1968). He suggested that your mind applies size constancy to the image so that you interpret the two-dimensional pattern in a three-dimensional way. It is assumed that when the arrows point outwards, you view it as you would the edge of a box; the mind thinks the corners are going away from you and so the line must be near you, and therefore shorter. In contrast, when the arrows point inwards you assume the arrows are going into the distance, that the line is further away, and therefore larger. This explanation has been challenged, as the same basic effect also happens when squares are used instead of the arrows. Nevertheless, it is still suggested that the illusion happens because our minds try to apply the rules of the three-dimensional world to these two-dimensional images (Howe and Purves, 2005).

A similar illusion, based on size constancy, is shown in Figure 5.8. This is known as the Ponzo illusion (Ponzo, 1913), and the task is simply to decide which of the two lines in the middle looks the longest. Decided yet? Again, conventional wisdom is that the top line is perceived as being longer. The explanation offered for this is that the long lines on the right and left make it look like

Figure 5.7: A version of the Müller-Lyer illusion (Müller-Lyer, 1889)

Figure 5.8: A version of the Ponzo illusion (Ponzo, 1913)

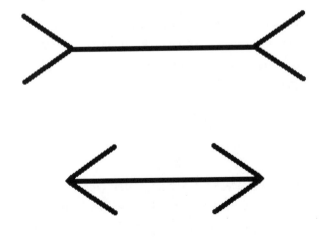

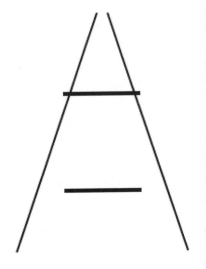

there is some depth (like train tracks or the side of the road). We know that things get smaller as they go away from us, so the top line must be longer than the bottom one. Again, this illusion relies on your mind interpreting the two-dimensional image in a three-dimensional way.

More recently, Kingdom et al. (2007) demonstrated another interesting illusion that, they suggested, is also based on size constancy. In their paper they presented pictures of the famous leaning tower of Pisa side by side (see Figure 5.9). Importantly, they were exactly the same picture. When viewed side by side the tower on the right appears to be leaning much more than the one on the left. Again, it is important to remember that they are the same picture. Kingdom et al. (2007) argue that our visual systems treat the two side-by-side pictures as part of the same scene. We know that two things that are parallel will come together (converge) as they go into the distance. Imagine looking down a long straight road. As the road gets further into the distance the sides of the road seem to get closer. When the two pictures are put next to each other they don't converge as you would expect, instead they are parallel. Confused, the mind decides that they cannot be *actually* parallel and so perceives one as moving away from the other. It remains to be seen if this explanation is sufficient, but you can create the illusion yourself with two pictures where the central objects go into the distance. The bigger the object, or the further the distance, the better this will be.

We have focused here upon the idea of size constancy because it is easy to demonstrate how this simple principle can be used to create mental illusions. The power of these illusions is in demonstrating to us that what we perceive is easily influenced by our minds in ways that we are

Figure 5.9: The leaning tower illusion (adapted with permission from Kingdom et al., 2007)

not aware of. Indeed, had I not revealed to you the 'truth' of the illusions, then they would not have been illusions at all, just how you perceived the world. Importantly, these constancies are a neat way of describing how we process things that exist in a three-dimensional world in terms of aspects such as size, shape and distances. But what about those patterns or objects that we perceive as having constant sizes or shapes? How is our mind processing them?

Critical thinking activity

Tricks of the mind

Critical thinking focus: critical and creative thinking

Key question: *What are the limits of the Müller-Lyer illusion?*

In this chapter you have learned about a particular visual illusion called the Müller-Lyer illusion (Müller-Lyer, 1889). The illusion is illustrated in Figure 5.7. The basic idea is that a line with inward-facing arrows appears to be longer than a line with outward- facing arrows. You have also learned that the exact explanation for this is still a matter for debate. One idea is that the mind may reinterpret the lines according to whether, in a three-dimensional world, they would represent the edge of something further away or nearer to you (Gregory, 1968). You have also learned that this explanation has been challenged because the same effect has occurred with the arrows replaced by other objects such as boxes (see Figure 5.10).

Part of the challenge that psychologists face is to understand all the ways in which something can be found. It is also important to work out all of those circumstances that make it difficult to find the same phenomenon. These are known as the **boundary conditions** of an effect because they set the boundaries of what we have to try to explain. In the case of the Müller-Lyer illusion, if we show that it works with boxes (rather than arrows), the boundaries of the explanation have to be able to move to include this. Alternatively, we need to have a good reason why it shouldn't be included – for example, that it is a different effect and requires a different explanation.

Figure 5.10: An alternative version of the Müller-Lyer illusion using boxes

An important property of boundary conditions is that, for any effect, no one knows what they all are! The more we discover, the more challenges it poses for our explanations but the better the explanations will be. Discovering these boundary conditions is a part of what makes science so exciting, and it requires a lot of thought and creativity on the part of the scientist. This activity is structured to help you to gain experience of thinking creatively about the boundaries of a psychological phenomenon.

The task itself is very simple. You will need a piece of paper with two lines of equal length drawn on it. You can do this using a pen, paper and a ruler, or a suitable computer program (e.g. Microsoft Word, Paint), paper and a printer. Once you have the lines, add something to the ends of them that may produce the illusion (or not). You have already seen the example of adding boxes. What would happen if you used curvy arrows? Or circles? This is all about your creativity, so let yourself get carried away. Just remember that the two versions need to be different from each other because the task is to judge the longest line (even though they are the same). Sometimes the effect may be very strong and you can tell straight away if it has worked. Other times you may have to ask friends or family to help you judge.

Repeat this as many times as you like. Each time you will find a new boundary condition so make sure you keep notes as you go along. When you run out of ideas, or are too tired to carry on, have a look at your notes and see what you have learned about the illusion. You will have an idea about what an explanation would have to include, and what it could possibly exclude (although you will never know for sure).

Critical thinking review

This activity helps develop your creative thinking skills while thinking about a psychological phenomenon. In particular, this gives you an opportunity to exercise your creative muscles while learning what it feels like to discover boundary conditions. This is very important because this type of knowledge helps guide how ideas are formed and developed. Being creative and innovative in exploring boundaries can not only reveal important challenges but also take research in new and inspirational directions.

Other skills you may have used in this activity include: analysing and evaluating; problem solving; decision making; information technology; and organisational skills.

Pattern/object recognition

While our minds must organise the light on our retinas into a coherent visual world, and handle changes in size, shape and distance, we often take for granted that we recognise the objects within it. For example, imagine that you visit a house you have never been to before. When you enter the living room and are asked to take a seat, you will be able to recognise something in the room that is a chair (and therefore suitable for sitting on). If you go into the kitchen and are asked to 'grab a mug', you should be able to identify a mug (as long as you find the right cupboard). Now I'm guessing that you find most of this pretty unremarkable. The idea that you can recognise a mug as a mug, even if you can't see the handle, may seem so trivial that you wonder why I'm mentioning it. Well, the simple fact is that researchers who have tried to explain this have not found it quite so easy.

In an ideal world we would begin our discussions by talking about three-dimensional objects, because these are what we perceive on a daily basis. However, because the task is much harder than you would think, we will start at a more basic level – how we recognise two-dimensional patterns.

Template approaches

We will begin by turning our attention to early proposals about object recognition that suggested that templates, or miniature copies, may be stored in our minds. Our sensations are then compared to these templates before recognising something. In other words, it is suggested that every pattern has a template for it in a permanent mental store, and that these templates are compared against patterns that we see until we establish a match – at which point the pattern is recognised.

A simple demonstration is to think about the two-dimensional patterns that are letters. In Chapter 4 you learned how words may be recognised. An even earlier part of this process is recognising the patterns in the first place – that is, recognising which letters are which. Here we will start at this very early stage of cognitive processing, from the ink on the page or the pixels on the screen to which letter is which. We will make it even simpler and just take the example of the letter 'f'. The template-matching approach suggests you have a template for the letter 'f' in a permanent mental store. When part of the image on the retina matches this template, you then recognise the letter 'f'. This idea sounds simple enough, but can you spot any problems? Consider all the different versions of 'f' in Figure 5.11.

You will notice in Figure 5.11 that the pattern of the letter 'f' varies according to the font it is in. To use a template approach you would need to have an exact template of each of these different patterns mentally stored so that you could recognise them as 'f'. We then have to remember that we are only thinking about 'f' and a small number of fonts. Think of all the letters in the alphabet, then all the numbers in the world, and you should begin to realise that the number of templates

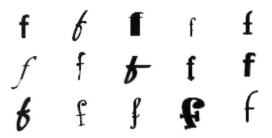

Figure 5.11: *The letter 'f' presented in fifteen different fonts*

needed increases very rapidly. Now, think of all possible variations of these patterns, and then do this for all the objects and patterns you may have encountered in your life. It should become obvious that a major issue for this approach is the very large number of templates that would be needed. This in itself is a minor limitation (it is implausible but possible) until you consider what happens when you see the same letter in a font you've never seen before. Do you fail to recognise the letter? It is unlikely. Instead you will probably recognise it to some extent even though you have never seen it presented in that particular way. By thinking about this approach you should have now learned that an important aspect of working out how we recognise patterns and objects is deciding how we deal with the large variety of visual appearances of the same pattern or object. It is widely held that suggesting an almost infinite number of very detailed templates is not the best solution.

Prototype approaches

If we assume we don't use templates, what is the alternative? Well, rather than having lots of different templates a mental representation could be stored that simply contained the key attributes that would define that object. We call this a prototype, and pattern recognition would take place through matching against the closest version.

Task — Pick an example of an object in your current location. Try to describe what the key characteristics a prototype of this object might need to have. Remember that the prototype you describe should be able to be used to identify all possible versions of this object, without mistaking it for another type of object. This may not be as easy as it sounds.

Based on the limitations you learned about previously, an advantage of this approach is that the permanent mental store would need far fewer prototypes than it would templates. This would make the approach more plausible, although this remains a subjective judgement on the part of researchers. What I mean by this is that we have no *real* idea as to the exact number of prototypes that would be needed, neither do we know how many would constitute plausible, and how many would constitute implausible. Nevertheless, it is commonly accepted among researchers within this area that the reduction in the number was an important step. However, a limitation with the prototype approach is that it is vague as to the exact processes that happen when trying to match a pattern to a prototype. In contrast, feature-detection models of perception are much less vague about this aspect.

Feature-detection approaches

An alternative to the storage of prototypes with key attributes is to have very specific lists of all of the features and their relations that define the object or pattern. This is known as a feature-detection approach. The role of the information processing is then to detect these features at increasingly sophisticated levels, and determine from them what the object is.

An early and influential model in this approach has been the pandemonium model described by Selfridge (1959). In this model the job of processing the information is carried out by 'demons'. Each of these demons looks for a particular feature, and they shout when they see it. Higher-level demons listen to these shouts as they try to detect features with particular relationships. They listen to the shouts of the demons below them and they shout themselves when they think these relations may be there. Even higher-level demons listen to these shouts and try to work out if the pattern they are trying to detect is there, based on the relations of the features (i.e. the demons shouting below them). If so, they shout too, and so on all the way to a demon at the top who decides what the object is. The result is pandemonium but the object, in theory, can be successfully identified from its visual appearance. It is worth noting that not all feature-detection models are described in terms of shouting demons, but it is a useful example when you are first learning about them.

As with all of the theories and approaches that you will learn about in this book, every new development creates a new set of questions and a new set of limitations. In terms of the prototype and feature-detection models of perception, the most important limitation to learn about is that they do not account for the circumstances at the time. You will remember that we referred to this as context. There can be an extrinsic context (aspects of the environment etc.) and an intrinsic context (aspects such as thoughts, intentions, emotions, memories). Context is important because the context in which we perceive something can often determine how quickly or easily we recognise it. For example, you will be better at recognising a loaf of bread on a kitchen counter than a mailbox or drum in the same position (e.g. Palmer, 1975). You will learn more about the importance of context when we discuss the top-down approach to perception. For now, it is sufficient to note that how to recognise two-dimensional patterns poses a challenge for researchers.

Skill builder activity

Beyond talk and text

Transferable skill focus: communication

Key question: *Can we visually communicate the ideas behind prototype approaches and feature-detection approaches?*

A major challenge any researcher faces is communicating their ideas in a way that other people understand. While you will be used to how cognitive psychologists try to communicate their ideas through writing about them, or talking about them in lectures or seminars, you may be surprised to learn that they also try to communicate their ideas visually, with more than just text, through presenting posters or even using websites. Just as researchers must develop their visual communication skills, this activity is an opportunity for you to develop these same skills.

This activity can be completed with either a piece of paper and pens, or on a computer using software that lets you manipulate text and its relative size, shape, colour and position (such as Microsoft® Publisher, Microsoft® Word or Microsoft® Paint). Your task is to design a poster that explains what a prototype approach to object recognition is, what a feature-detection approach is, and what the limitations are. What these approaches are, and their limitations, have been briefly described on the previous pages.

Your challenge is to try to communicate these ideas visually, with as little writing as possible. Remember, part of the challenge is to complete this activity using more than just text, so think about what drawings you could use and how they could communicate the ideas. For example, you may want to try drawing an object in the middle of the page and then illustrating how the information would be processed according to both approaches. Alternatively, you may want to actually draw the demons in the pandemonium model – along with all their shouting. Try to be ambitious and be happy to make mistakes. If you want to make use of colour, then go for it – there are no limits.

Once you have done your first version of the poster, have a look and see if there are any changes you want to make. Did you make the right decisions? Did it work out as you expected? Now do a second version, making any changes you want, or simply make corrections to the first version. Continue this process until you are happy with the final design and how you have communicated the ideas.

Skill builder review

This activity helps develop your visual communication skills. When communicating any ideas we often choose between writing about them or talking about them, yet using visual communication (other than text) can sometimes be more effective. Being able to communicate your ideas in different ways is important because different people have different preferences about how ideas are communicated to them, and can sometimes grasp some ideas more easily when presented visually. By taking advantage of the different ways of communicating available to you, you should find that you get your ideas across more effectively and to a wider audience.

Other skills you may have used in this activity include: information technology; organisational skills; and decision making.

3-D object recognition

You have learned that what is an effortless task for humans, perceiving and recognising objects, still poses a considerable challenge to researchers. You have also learned that many early approaches to this issue have struggled to fully account for recognising something as simple as a letter on a page. But what about objects that are three-dimensional? An issue for many researchers specifically interested in recognition of three-dimensional objects is whether processes of recognition in the mind are view-based or view invariant (also known as object-based).

A view-invariant approach argues that processing occurs in such a way that at the end of it we have a three-dimensional mental representation (e.g. Biederman, 1987; Marr and Nishihara, 1978). In theory, this can be mentally turned to determine if it matches objects that we are looking at. An important argument for this approach is that this helps us recognise an object from any viewpoint, even if we have never seen it from that angle before. While this may seem reasonable, you may also be interested to learn that research has demonstrated that we aren't that good at recognising objects from many different viewpoints (e.g. Bülthoff and Edelman, 1992), despite what we might think. The implication for how we recognise objects is that the information processing may not be independent of the point of view from which we are looking at that object; instead it may be viewpoint dependent.

A view-based approach to this issue proposes that we do not store and use three-dimensional models of objects in our minds; instead, we store two-dimensional representations from different angles (e.g. Logothetis et al., 1995). Objects are recognised on the basis of these two-dimensional viewpoints, rather than a more abstract three-dimensional model. Like the template approach you learned about above, such an approach may be criticised because it requires considerable storage of many different representations. Some researchers have got around this problem by suggesting ways in which two-dimensional representations can be generalised using only a small number of these view-based representations (e.g. Ullman, 1998). As with other aspects of cognitive psychology, the most appropriate approach to three-dimensional object recognition remains an active and developing area.

Approaches to perception

In this chapter you have learned about how our minds might organise our visual world, what rules they might apply as images on the retina change in size and shape, and how these changing images might be recognised as patterns or objects. To complete our learning, for now, we will finish off by thinking about things at a slightly higher level and address a more fundamental question. We have considered throughout this chapter that the mind processes information from the world to create our perceptions. But is this really necessary? Can we perceive what we need to know directly? Or do our expectations and ideas about the world need to influence what we perceive? These two approaches to processing information in perception are known as **bottom-up processing** and **top-down processing**.

Bottom-up processing

In the 'bottom-up' approach to processing it is assumed that perceptions are constructed from the outside-in. The most extreme version of this approach is to assume that the information provided by the environment is so good that no processing is needed at all. This is a view that was expressed by Gibson (1966, 1979) and is known as the Gibsonian approach to perception. Indeed, it has received many labels to the extent that it is also known as: direct perception; the ecological approach; and data-driven processing. While there may be fine distinctions between the exact meanings of these terms, it is perhaps most useful to learn about what makes Gibson's approach particularly controversial for some researchers.

Gibson (1979) suggested an idea that he called 'affordances'. To best understand affordances we will take the example of recognising an object again. The more traditional view is that the nature and purpose of an object is analysed and determined in the mind. That is, once it is recognised you might remember what it is for or what its purpose is. In contrast, the idea of 'affordances' is that this information is provided directly by the object itself through the sensations it creates. For example, the traditional approach would suggest that we analyse the curve and colour of the image of a banana to determine what it is, a banana. At that point we may remember that a banana is for eating, and we act accordingly (potentially, eat it). The idea of an affordance is that the visual information that the banana provides gives us all the information that is needed to know that we can eat it – it 'affords' being eaten. Central to this is the idea that perception and action are directly linked. There are no roles for other cognitive processes such as memory, so prior experience would have no influence at all on how you perceive things. If you are struggling getting your head around this concept, then you are not alone, and it is the reason why it is seen as so controversial. However, in the interests of considering every relevant viewpoint, it is one worth considering.

In general, the difficulties for such an approach are the errors we make with visual illusions and the influences of context. If all the information is afforded by the environment, why do we make mistakes? The answer to this question is unclear, and the mainstream of psychological research on visual perception has approached things in a slightly different way.

Top-down processing

You have learned already that the bottom-up approach is data-driven in the sense that the patterns of light result in objects being perceived directly. The term 'top-down' is used to talk about an approach to visual perception in which our expectations about the world help us interpret these instead (e.g. Bruner, 1957; Gregory, 1972). So the perception is not completely determined by the patterns of light but also by influential higher level representations such as memories. Where the previous approach was 'data-driven' the suggestion here is that it may instead be concept-driven processing.

Task — Explain, in your own words, the difference between top-down processing and bottom-up processing. Use an example of perceiving the face of a familiar friend to demonstrate your thoughts.

So why might we believe that perception is concept-driven? As with much of the evidence presented in this chapter, simple demonstrations may be all that is needed. One of the easiest demonstrations is to think about what happens when something is obscured.

In Figure 5.12 a sentence is shown but a few letters have been obscured. Previously, these blobs have been described as ink blots, but in the digital age it is not clear what the excuse is – perhaps the computer is faulty. Can you still read the sentence? Hopefully you can. Indeed, I shouldn't have to hope at all as I am relying on the idea that your mind will 'fill in the gaps'. That is to say, your expectations about the world are helping you interpret these patterns of black against white. Letters are being recognised that you can't actually see, or you cannot see all the features of, and the context is being used to resolve particular issues. For example, the eighth word could be either *hot* or *hat* but a *hat* makes sense in this sentence – you probably didn't even feel as if you paused to decide. That we automatically, and with little conscious thought, resolve these discrepancies is, of course, important; however, it is just as important that sometimes our minds mislead us when presented with a visual illusion. Indeed, the important aspect of the illusion is

The time had come to wear her hat outside.

Figure 5.12:
An obscured sentence

that it seems real when it actually isn't. This demonstrates that additional top-down processing is needed at some stage. Not everything that makes up our visual experience is perceived directly from the information in the environment. Gregory (1980) characterised it in the way that we are constantly hypothesis testing. Faced with ambiguous information, we test the ideas we have about the way the world should be, and if they fit with the limited information we have, then we tend to accept them. In general, this is a very efficient way of doing things, but sometimes we get caught out.

Assignments

1. Describe two visual illusions and explain what they tell us about visual perception. State the basic ideas behind both illusions, and use further examples and analogies from real life to illustrate your thoughts.

2. Evaluate two different theories of object recognition. Describe, with examples, the basic ideas behind both theories. Explain the strengths and weaknesses of both theories, and argue for which provides the most complete explanation.

3. Compare and contrast top-down processing and bottom-up processing as approaches to understanding perception. Provide examples (real or made up) and explain how both approaches might be used to explain our perceptions of them.

Summary: what you have learned

You have learned that our minds need to organise the information from our senses to help understand the world. Laws of perceptual organisation do a good job of describing these, and several have been proposed. They include: proximity; similarity; closure; good continuation; and connectedness.

You now know that there are certain rules about our visual world that our minds use to interpret the two-dimensional images on the retina in a three-dimensional way. These include constancies such as size and shape, as well as the relationship between size, shape and distance. Interestingly, the mind can be tricked with what we call visual illusions. You have learned about three of these that take advantage of size constancy: the Müller-Lyer illusion; the Ponzo illusion; and the leaning tower illusion.

You have also learned about different approaches to understanding how we recognise specific patterns and objects. Researchers have struggled to create a system that can recognise objects and patterns in different forms, and from different angles. You have learned about template, prototype and feature-detection models as potential solutions for this.

Finally, you now know that psychologists distinguish between top-down processing and bottom-up processing. You have learned that top-down processing is driven by concepts and previous experiences, while bottom-up processing is driven by the information on the retina (the data).

Within this chapter you have had an opportunity to develop your critical and creative thinking skills through exploring the boundary conditions of the Müller-Lyer illusion. You have also had the opportunity to develop your visual communication skills through designing a poster about object recognition.

Further reading

Findlay, JM and Gilchrist, ID (2003) *Active vision: the psychology of looking and seeing.* Oxford: Oxford University Press.

An important account of visual perception that informs the reader about the active processes of looking in addition to the more passive processes of seeing.

Hatfield, G (2009) *Perception and cognition: essays in the philosophy of psychology.* Oxford: Oxford University Press.

An in-depth look into both the psychological and philosophical issues surrounding our understanding of how we see.

Mather, G (2011) *An introduction to sensation and perception.* London: Routledge.

An extended introduction to sensation and perception that integrates information on all of the five senses in an accessible way.

Chapter 6

Attention

Learning outcomes

By the end of this chapter you should:

- *be able to describe the nature of divided attention;*
- *be able to summarise different ideas about the selectivity of attention;*
- *be able to discuss whether attention can be shared over several locations; and*
- *be able to analyse, evaluate and make decisions about claims using evidence.*

Introduction

What are you paying attention to right now? Hopefully, you are paying attention to the words on this page. Indeed, I am very confident that you are attending to each of these words to try to make sense of this chapter. These words are not the only form of information your mind could be dealing with at the moment. Unless you are on a desert island, then there are probably many different noises around you – perhaps the traffic outside your window, the banging of doors, the hum of a fridge, or you may even have the television on while reading this. It isn't just these sounds that your mind could be processing: you may have an itch on your neck, and then there is the feel of your clothes against your skin, or even the feel of your hair against your forehead.

Task — Take a second to make a list of every type of information you could pay attention to at the moment; for example, you could be listening to someone's conversation and looking at the colours in the sky. Try to write down as much as you can.

In general, we are constantly bombarded with information to our senses – from touch and sound to sights and smells. Interestingly, our conscious experience is of paying attention to only a small amount of this information. When cognitive psychologists study attention, they are interested in many questions about this, from what we choose to attend to, and when we choose to attend to it, through to attending to many different things at once.

In this chapter you will first learn about how well we can divide our attention between different things. This dividing up of our attention we will call divided attention (for obvious reasons). You will also learn about how we ignore irrelevant information and select other information. We will call this selective attention. Finally, we will focus in detail on attention for specific positions or locations. You will learn about interesting evidence that suggests we can pay attention to different locations at the same time. However, you must first learn about the basic questions asked about attention. We will start with this one: can I pay attention to more than one thing?

Divided attention

While we could pay attention to a lot of different sources of information, we are consciously aware of paying attention to much less. You don't need a lot of scientific evidence to accept that we don't pay attention to absolutely everything all at once. We can rule that idea out fairly quickly. We can also rule out the idea that we pay attention to nothing at all. This leaves us in an interesting position. We know we don't pay attention to everything, and that we don't pay attention to nothing. We are therefore left with the idea of 'something in-between'. This 'something in-between' allows us to do several tasks at once but not be overwhelmed by attending to everything. Some people call this multitasking. If you have ever tried to do several tasks at once, you will know already that it is not always easy to split your attention between them, and you may often miss stuff. You may find it easy to doodle and listen to a telephone conversation, but find it more difficult to listen to the radio and read a book. Working out how we multitask and what information we miss in what conditions has led to some fascinating findings.

Influences on divided attention

One important property that determines whether we can divide our attention between tasks is the similarity of the tasks to each other. For example, people have difficulty following two streams of speech at the same time when presented separately over a pair of headphones (Allport et al., 1972). This is like trying to listen to two people speaking to you at exactly the same time. When one of the streams of speech is presented visually, and the other is presented over the headphones, participants remembered the unattended visual stream much better. Performance on this task is therefore improved by presenting the information in two different ways (visual and auditory), rather than both in the same way (both auditory). Performance is also influenced by similarities in the types of response that are needed (e.g. McLeod, 1977) or similarity in terms of the type of cognitive processes that will be used after attention is allocated to them (Wickens, 1984).

Another important property is the difficulty of the two tasks. For example, Sullivan (1976) adapted the listening experiments above and varied the difficulty of the stream that participants were asked to focus upon. The stream that participants are asked to focus upon is known as the stream that is being shadowed. When the stream being shadowed was made more relevant, participants found it harder to detect specific target words in the stream they weren't specifically listening to. However, while there is evidence that both task similarity and task difficulty influence the ability to divide attention, researchers have found that the effect of similarity can have a greater impact than that of task difficulty (e.g. Segal and Fusella, 1970).

Practice is also widely accepted as important for divided attention tasks. That is to say, if you cannot divide your attention between two tasks the first time you try, it doesn't mean it will not be possible once you have had lots of practice. The seminal study demonstrating this property of divided attention was conducted by Spelke et al. (1976). They asked their participants to read and understand short stories while also writing down words that were dictated to them. While poor at this initially, repeated practice over 30 hours led to a clear improvement in their performance. Similar evidence was presented by Shaffer (1975), although it is worth noting that while there is improvement in these sorts of divided attention tasks, performance is rarely as good as when they are performed individually (see Broadbent, 1982).

Task ── Make a note of two tasks that you regularly do at the same time. For example, you might walk and listen to music at the same time. Reflect on whether similarity, difficulty or practice has the biggest impact on your ability to do these tasks.

An example from everyday experience is the use of hands-free speakers so that drivers can have telephone conversations in the car. In the UK, in 2003, it was made a motoring offence to use a mobile phone while driving a car. This applied specifically to hand-held devices but not immediately to those considered as hands-free. If a police officer thought you weren't in control of the car while on a hands-free phone, then they could issue a motoring conviction for this, although this judgement is, of course, subjective. So why is this important? Well, it raises an interesting question about attention. One assumption here is that by not holding a phone when having a conversation, a driver will drive more safely. Being able to pay attention is part of driving safely, and research suggests that dividing attention, regardless of whether you are holding the phone, can still impact on driving ability (e.g. Alm and Nilsson, 1994).

Researchers have looked at whether dividing attention between driving and having a conversation can affect performance in a driving simulator. It has been found that when using a mobile phone, participants take longer to respond to changes and are less likely to detect the slowing down of a car in front (e.g. Lamble et al., 1999; Garcia-Larrea et al., 2001). Interestingly, slower reaction times and generally poorer performance have been found at equivalent levels regardless of whether the conversation is over the telephone or with someone in the car, when compared to no conversation at all (Amado and Ulupinar, 2005; Collett et al., 2009; Gugerty et al., 2004). Together with other research, this suggests that the performance of any tasks in addition to driving may have a detrimental effect (see Collett et al., 2010 for a review). However, it is noteworthy that passengers will often stop conversation when in the car if they feel that the driver needs to concentrate on the road, something that doesn't happen with conversations over mobile phones (Crundall et al., 2005).

Critical thinking activity

Driving to distraction

Critical thinking focus: analysing and evaluating

Key question: *What makes talking while driving hard?*

In this activity you will be encouraged to analyse and evaluate the following claim: *I can pay attention to driving while using my mobile phone because they're not the same thing*.

Your task is to decide whether this claim is supported by the available evidence from cognitive psychology. You have learned already that our ability to divide attention is influenced by at least three things: task similarity; task difficulty; and practice. The above quote implies that the person believes they can divide attention between the tasks because they are not similar. However, they are neglecting the ideas of task difficulty and practice.

To help you to complete this task you should use the brief descriptions of previous research that have been presented in this chapter. One challenge you will face if/when you read about psychology is that the author may be writing about something slightly different from the question you're trying to answer – for example, this chapter was not written to specifically address the claim above. However, there is enough information here to begin to do so. Your challenge as a critical thinker is to extract the relevant information and organise it in a way that helps you to evaluate the claim.

To help you extract the appropriate information, I suggest you draw a table on a piece of paper (or use a word processor). You will need at least three rows – one each for *similarity*, *difficulty* and *practice*. In the first column label each row as: similarity; difficulty; practice. In the second column leave enough room to put in a little about the evidence that each of these influences divided attention. Finally, leave a third column where you can write in how each influence might apply to this specific example of driving.

Complete the table using the information you have here. Once you have completed the table, write a short statement (around 500 words) that gives an overall evaluation of the claim, as well as providing the reasoning. If you feel adventurous, read other textbooks or journal articles to see if you can fill out more information in each column. You may find that this changes your overall analysis.

Critical thinking review

This activity helps develop your analysis and evaluation skills in relation to how we can judge claims using available evidence. You were encouraged to organise the information you had in order to complete the evaluation. This sort of organisation is an important part of completing any structured analysis and evaluation.

You have learned throughout this book that we have limited cognitive resources, so it is often helpful to use something external to organise your thoughts when completing any evaluation (e.g. a piece of paper or a word processing document). This also helps you visualise the arguments in your analysis in a different way, something that is an important part of problem solving. In the 'real world' such skills are crucial in making sense of the claims that others make in an informed and intelligent way, not just in your academic study.

Other skills you may have used in this activity: organisational skills; critical thinking; decision making; and problem solving.

It is clear that we have a limited capacity for doing two tasks at once, which can be influenced by, among other things, task similarity, task difficulty and practice. These influences are important on their own, but it is interesting to think about what this tells us about the capacity of attention in general. In other words, we know it is limited but in what ways?

Single vs. multiple capacities

An early approach to understanding attentional capacity was to suggest that there is one overall capacity. In other words, we have a set number of resources that all tasks can make use of, but we have only enough to do a few tasks at a time (e.g. Norman and Bobrow, 1975). It was suggested by Kahneman (1973) that what we allocate attention to is then determined by several additional factors such as: how much energy we have; the type of person we are; and what is relevant in that moment. Importantly, these approaches assume a central resource that is limited but can be used for all types of task. We will refer to this idea as a single general capacity.

This approach is useful when trying to explain why we struggle to do multiple tasks at once. In particular, it provides a simple reason as to why task difficulty is so important. Difficult tasks require more resources, the resources are limited, therefore there are not enough resources to do lots of difficult tasks. This can also, tentatively, explain why practice improves performance, if we assume that practice makes the tasks 'less difficult' (e.g. Shiffrin and Schneider, 1977). The logic then follows that for difficult tasks practice makes the tasks less difficult (some may say automatic), therefore fewer resources are needed, so attention can be divided among more tasks. Unfortunately, it is not as easy to explain the influence of task similarity. There is no clear reason, if we use a set of central resources, why it is easier to divide attention between two dissimilar tasks.

Task — In your own words, write down why a general capacity approach can explain the influence of task difficulty and the influence of practice, but cannot be used to explain the influence of task similarity.

The alternative position is one in which there are multiple capacities (e.g. Allport, 1980; Navon and Gopher, 1979). In this approach it is assumed that the type of information being processed is important. You have learned already that when people receive information in different **modalities** it is easier to divide attention between them, than when the information is provided in the same modality (e.g. Allport et al., 1972). This could be explained if there are several different specific processing mechanisms, and they have their own capacity (e.g. Allport, 1980). If you have different mechanisms for different modalities, then it is not surprising that it is easier to divide attention between listening to a message and reading a message, than it is to divide attention between listening to two messages. It is therefore likely that we have multiple different capacities of resources that are used for different types of task.

Selective attention

In the previous section you learned about dividing your attention between two tasks. This is not the only way we use attention. Sometimes we may want to focus on one thing, ignoring everything else. In other words, we may want to be very selective about what we pay attention to. For example, we may want to listen to a new track on our music player, ignoring everything else that is happening in the room. Studying how we selectively focus on one thing is known as the study of either focused attention or selective attention. We will use the second term here but they refer to broadly the same thing.

You may have worked out already that research on attention has a longer history than research on other aspects of cognitive psychology. We must therefore return to seminal work reported in the 1950s when we first learn about selective attention. More specifically, we must learn about research undertaken by Cherry (1953) using a task that is known as the dichotic listening task.

The dichotic listening task was one of a series of experiments reported by Cherry (1953), but its implications have led it to become the most famous. In this experiment, Cherry asked his participants to listen to two messages over a pair of headphones. Both messages were read by the same speaker and presented at the same time. The main difference between the messages was that one was presented to the left ear, while the other was presented to the right ear. The participant was asked to listen to and repeat back, out loud, one of the messages (either the left or the right). The participants found this task very easy. Interestingly, when asked about what had been presented in the other ear, the ear they were not listening to, participants reported very little information. Indeed, the only things they could remember were some of the physical characteristics, such as whether it was a man or a woman speaking.

So why is this interesting? This research raised the question of *when* we select the information we are choosing to attend to, or more importantly, when we select the information we won't pay attention to. Why did the participants know so little about the message they weren't attending to? Do we select an information source before we know what it consists of? Or do we select it after we have processed at least something about it (such as its meaning)? Different researchers have suggested that we selectively attend to things early on (e.g. Broadbent, 1958; Treisman, 1960, 1964) based on things such as its physical characteristics (e.g. which ear it is in). However, other researchers have suggested that we do this at a much later stage (e.g. Deutsch and Deutsch, 1963; Norman, 1968) perhaps after we have processed something of what it is (such as what the words are). Theoretical models that assume the selection is made early on are known as early selection models. Similarly, theoretical models that assume the selection is made later on are known as late selection models. Both types of model have been argued for strongly.

Early vs. late selection

Broadbent (1958) provided one of the first theoretical explanations of the dichotic listening task. Broadbent suggested that information processing made use of a filter. He argued that information about the different stimulation from the environment is first stored in a temporary form, which he referred to as the sensory buffer. To stop the system from being overloaded, not everything is then processed. Instead, a filter selectively allows through some information for further processing. This further processing may involve analysing it for meaning. The dichotic listening task is therefore completed by selecting the message based on a simple sensory property – the location of the sounds (left ear or right ear). Once selected, the information passes through the filter, and it is only then that it is analysed for its meaning.

Treisman (1960, 1964) proposed a variation on this type of model. This was needed because of a sequence of results from other researchers that had begun to cast doubt on the basic assumptions of Broadbent's (1958) model (e.g. Gray and Wedderburn, 1960). The model proposed by Treisman (1960, 1964) is referred to as the attenuation model. This is because it assumes that the unattended information is attenuated. But what does this mean?

An assumption of Broadbent's (1958) original model is that the information that wasn't given any attention remained in the sensory buffer. It was suggested that information in this buffer disappeared rapidly and that it was essentially lost. In contrast, Treisman (1960, 1964) suggested that a small amount of the information did get through the filter, although in a very weakened form.

The alternative to these two ideas is to suggest that the selection occurs at a much later stage (late selection). This perspective requires that information is analysed for its meaning before it is selected (e.g. Deutsch and Deutsch, 1963; Norman, 1968). It is argued that selection occurs based on what is considered most relevant or most important as a result of this analysis of meaning. Interestingly, it is argued that the information is only passed into conscious awareness at this point so the analysis based on meanings is considered to be largely unconscious.

Task — Compare and contrast early selection models of selective attention and late selection models of selective attention. On a piece of paper make two lists of the main points about both models. Use arrows or highlighters to draw attention to similarities and differences in the two lists.

Johnston and Heinz (1978) highlighted one difficulty with resolving the differences between these two approaches. This difficulty was that both approaches were inflexible. They argued that the selection of attention may be more flexible than supposed, potentially occurring in two different modes (an early mode and a late mode). An alternative approach has been taken more recently with load theory (Lavie, 1995, 2000; Lavie et al., 2004). Rather than differentiate between early selection and late selection, load theory (e.g. Lavie et al., 2004) differentiates between perceptual selection and cognitive selection.

Load theory

Load theory suggests that selective attention involves both a perceptual selection mechanism and a cognitive selection mechanism. Selection occurs depending upon the 'load' that each of these has.

It is argued that the perceptual mechanism (Lavie and Tsal, 1994; Lavie, 1995) is relatively passive; it is not something that is under the control of our conscious awareness. In other words, it does its job without us feeling that we have any influence on it. With this mechanism, some of what is perceived is 'selected out' on the basis that there are simply not enough resources to attend to it all. This is referred to as having 'high perceptual load' and is analogous to when lots of information comes into the senses. In contrast, when there is not much going on (low perceptual load), then irrelevant information might be attended to as well because there are enough resources to do so.

In essence, this assumes that we will try to attend to as much perceptual information as possible, but will prioritise relevant stuff if there is a lot of it. This prioritising is not under our conscious control and is something that just happens.

Lavie and Tsal (1994) argued that perceptual load may in part explain why there is considerable evidence for both early selection models and late selection models. In their review of the available literature they suggested that examples of early selection occurred because the perceptual load was high in these experiments. There was so much information that there were no spare resources to allocate to the unattended information. Hence it looked as if the task-relevant information was chosen to be attended to early on. By comparison, they suggested that tasks that demonstrated late selection could be explained because they had low perceptual load. There were enough resources spare that the unattended information could be processed to some extent, but not fully. However, perceptual load alone is not sufficient to explain all of the available results. Lavie et al. (2004) also proposed a higher cognitive mechanism of selection.

The cognitive selection mechanism is considered as a relatively active mechanism that requires some resources to operate. This is when we 'choose' to attend to something based upon higher cognitive processes (such as memory demands or reasoning), and we have conscious experience of doing so. The selection by the two mechanisms therefore comes in a strict order. The perceptual mechanism is thought to be used first, while the cognitive mechanism is thought to be used *after* any selection by the perceptual mechanism. The cognitive mechanism is therefore most important when the perceptual load is low, because irrelevant information may also be receiving attention. In load theory, the role of the cognitive mechanism is to consciously attend to the relevant information, ignoring the other stuff.

Task — On a piece of paper, summarise the purpose of the cognitive mechanism and the purpose of the perceptual mechanism in load theory.

With the proposed cognitive mechanism the cognitive 'load' is also important. If our higher cognitive processes are occupied with completing difficult tasks, or storing lots of information, then the cognitive load is high. In contrast, if we are not doing anything else and the task is simple, then the cognitive load is low. It is suggested that having a low cognitive load allows us to use some of our resources to consciously select what we want to attend to, making it easier to ignore irrelevant information. By comparison, when we have a high cognitive load we find it more difficult to ignore irrelevant information because we do not have the resources to commit to actively selecting relevant information.

These predictions were supported by a series of experiments in which the level of perceptual load (high/low) and cognitive load (high/low) was manipulated (Lavie et al., 2004). Nevertheless, the principles of load theory have been challenged. Eltiti et al. (2005) demonstrated attention to distractors when they were highly salient, but under high perceptual load. Furthermore, Fitousi and Wenger (2011) have provided evidence against the assumption that the perceptual mechanism and the cognitive mechanism have different resources available to them. Importantly, considerations around load theory have opened up a new way to think about, and talk about, selective attention and have engaged researchers with a new set of problems.

Skill builder activity

A load in your mind

Transferable skill focus: decision making

Key question: *What predictions can we make about selective attention using load theory?*

In everyday life we always have to make decisions. In an ideal world we might weigh up the evidence for different scenarios and assess our decisions against some criteria. The decision that best meets the criteria is, in theory, the best available decision. Now we all know life is not quite like that, but when we try to make decisions in cognitive psychology, then it is important we are as rigorous as possible.

One decision we often have to make is whether evidence supports an idea or theory. What I mean by this is that researchers can do studies, and the results can be interesting, but the really interesting thing is whether it supports an idea about *how* our minds work. This skill builder will give you some practice in developing your decision-making skills in this context.

Presented below is some evidence from four fictional studies. Your task is to decide if they support load theory or not. If you cannot remember what load theory is, then review this chapter to remind yourself. We will start with the made-up findings.

Study 1: The task involved a high perceptual load, but a low cognitive load. The results indicated that participants did not pay attention to irrelevant distractions.

Study 2: The task involved a low perceptual load, but a high cognitive load. The results indicated that participants paid a lot of attention to the irrelevant distractions.

Study 3: The task involved a low perceptual load and a low cognitive load. The results indicated that participants paid little attention to the irrelevant distractions.

Study 4: The task involved a high perceptual load and a high cognitive load. The results indicated that participants paid lots of attention to the irrelevant distractors.

If you have read through the findings above, you may already feel overwhelmed in terms of how you would be able to interpret these. The key to deciding if these findings support the theory is to have a clear idea of what the theory would predict.

On a piece of paper, or in a word processing document, draw a 2 × 2 table – that is, a table with two rows and two columns. Across the top write 'perceptual load' and label the first column 'high' and the second column 'low'. Down the side write 'cognitive load' and label the first row 'high' and the second row 'low'. Your task is to complete the boxes in the table with the predictions (based on load theory). For example, if the perceptual load is high, and the cognitive load is low, then you would expect people to be able to be selective with their attention (ignore distractors). I will leave you to work out the other combinations. Once you have completed the table, use it to work out which of the above studies supports load theory.

Skill builder review

This activity helps develop your experience of making decisions about the relationship between research findings and theory in a systematic way. If you have completed the activity correctly, then you will realise that only three out of the four studies supported load theory. The study that did not support load theory was Study 4. If there is a high perceptual load, then you would not expect participants to be easily distracted because there may not be enough perceptual resources available to attend to the distractors. By presenting the thought processes on paper in a systematic way, I hope that the decision-making process seemed easier than when you first read about it.

Other skills you may have used in this activity include: understanding and using data; problem solving; and organisational skills.

Spatial attention

You have learned already that there are many sources of information that could be attended to, from touch and sound to sights and smells. One area that has been particularly well studied is that of spatial attention (e.g. Posner, 1978). Spatial attention can be taken to refer to at least two different ideas. First, it could refer to the way in which things (objects, letters, etc.) are related to each other in space – which ones are near each other, how far apart they are etc. Second, it could refer to focusing attention on a particular location or position. We will focus on the visual properties of space (visual location), and you will learn more specifically about visual spatial attention.

Attention and visual scenes

The first question to ask is why we might be interested in visual spatial attention at all. Have a quick look up from this book, and then come back to it and continue reading. Make sure you have a good look around. Now, what you were just looking at is what we will call a visual scene. Depending on where you are, there would have been objects (e.g. chairs, tables, books, magazines) and some backgrounds (e.g. walls, windows). The idea is that we don't consciously pay attention to everything in a scene all at once. If you have ever completed a puzzle of 'spot the difference', then you will already have some insight into this. 'Spot the difference' is a puzzle in which two almost identical pictures are presented next to each other and you have to circle (or highlight) the differences between them. Even though the two pictures are next to each other, it can still be tiresome and frustrating finding all the differences. Indeed, you may try to complete it by systematically 'paying attention' to different parts of the picture and comparing these parts. Keep this idea in mind as you continue to read through this chapter.

You may be interested to know that we believe that very early processing of visual scenes occurs across the whole scene and that there are few capacity limits to it (e.g. Sagi and Julesz, 1985). Later processing – for example, when we analyse things for meaning, such as finding differences between pictures – occurs in a much more restricted way and focuses on individual aspects of the scene. More specifically, the traditional view is that our attention is focused on a restricted area of space and cannot be divided between many different places (e.g. Eriksen and Eriksen, 1974; Posner, 1980; Broadbent, 1982; Posner et al., 1980).

Jans et al. (2010) have noted that there has been a rapid change in how we think about visual spatial attention in the ten years between 1998 and 2008. In particular, there has been a clear change in how we think our attention is focused in areas of space.

Spotlights and zoom lenses

Early ideas about the focus of visual spatial attention relied on the use of analogies. An analogy is when we compare two things as being similar to try to explain the properties of one of them. This is particularly useful in science as it allows researchers to use something that people know about to try to explain an idea that they may not be familiar with. When using analogies, it is, of course, important to remember that they are a means of making an idea clearer and are not a claim that something is *exactly the same*. An early analogy used in this area of cognitive psychology is that visual spatial attention is like a spotlight (e.g. Posner, 1980).

Imagine you are in a completely dark room full of objects. In your hands you have a torch, and you can shine it around the room. Wherever the light falls you can clearly see what is there (it is a powerful torch). The suggestion with the analogy between visual spatial attention and a spotlight is that they act in very similar ways. Attention is paid to a small area in our visual field, and it can be moved about to focus on different things. Initial evidence for this approach came from a series of studies by Posner and colleagues (e.g. Posner 1978, 1980; Posner et al., 1980).

This idea of a spotlight of attention was built upon by Eriksen and St James (1986) who used another analogy. They suggested that visual spatial attention was like a zoom lens, the kind of thing you would find on a camera. Just like a zoom lens on a camera, it was suggested that we can 'zoom in' to a smaller area in space, or 'zoom out' to larger areas of space. Like the spotlight model, this zoom lens model (Eriksen and St James, 1986) assumes that a single area of space is the focus of attention, although this area can change in size and position.

Split attention

Ideas such as having a spotlight or a zoom lens can be more broadly called unified models of attentional focus. This is because they work on the assumption that at any moment in time our attention is focused on only one area of space. The alternative view is that our attention can be spread across different regions of visual space at the same time. We will refer to this as multiple spotlights (e.g. Awh and Pashler, 2000; Kramer and Hahn, 1995) or split attention. This approach has received considerable support from experimental studies since the mid-1990s. One of the first of these was reported by Awh and Pashler (2000).

Awh and Pashler (2000) presented their participants with a visual display. This display was divided into 25 sections using a 5×5 square grid. Across these 25 locations, 23 different letters were presented along with two different numbers. The main task for the participants was to report what the numbers in the display were (e.g. 5 and 7) from among all the letters.

Just before each display was seen the participants saw cues on the screen as to the possible locations of the numbers. These cues were correct 80 per cent of the time – they were in the locations where the numbers were actually shown. These cues were therefore called valid cues. The cues that were given were not correct 20 per cent of the time – they were not in the locations where the numbers were actually shown. These cues were therefore called invalid cues. The most interesting conditions were the invalid cue conditions where the number was actually presented in a location that was in the middle of the two cues. Awh and Pashler (2000) found that performance was generally worse when the number was in between the cues than when it was exactly where the cues suggested. So why is this important?

If we assume a 'zoom lens' model, then this result is unexpected. We would have assumed that attention was spread across the two locations by 'zooming out' until both of them were within the focus of attention. If this was true, then anything 'in between' would also fall within the focus and be attended to as much as anything at the two locations. You therefore would not expect performance to be any different when the number was 'in between'. However, we would expect performance to be worse with this 'in between' location if attention was split between the two locations (and nothing in between). This split attention account has subsequently received considerable support (McMains and Sommers, 2004; Müller et al., 2003).

Overall, then, we have moved from considering attention to be allocated to one region of space to learning that it can be split between at least two different locations. Of course, it is also possible that both approaches represent different 'modes' of how attention works. Jans et al. (2010) argue that it is important to note that splitting attention across two or more locations comes at a cost to processing resources. They suggest that in normal circumstances it is easier, and more sensible, to pay attention to single locations. In other words, that the unified model of attention may represent the 'default' mode of allocating attention, but that multiple locations can be attended to if needed.

Task — In your own words, summarise the main differences between a 'zoom lens' model of focused visual attention and split attention models. Explain how these lead to different predictions about behaviour.

In this chapter we have focused on the processing of basic stimuli and how attention may be allocated to them. The real situation is, of course, more complex than this, with the 3-D world consisting of much more than the simple 2-D displays that have been used in these experiments. Furthermore, there is still a lot to learn about how attention is related to actions (not just perception), as well as its relationship to other cognitive processes such as memory and reasoning, and there are important questions to ask about 'what' attention is paid to, as well as when and where. If these topics interest you, then more information can be found in the further reading. Throughout this chapter we have also touched upon issues of conscious awareness. You can learn more about these issues in Chapter 7.

Assignments

1. Describe some of the influences that task similarity, task difficulty and practice can have on divided attention.

2. Compare and contrast early selection models and late selection models of attention. Discuss an alternative approach that may resolve any differences.

3. Evaluate the differences between 'spotlight', 'zoom lens' and split attention models of visual spatial attention. Describe the basic differences between the approaches, and consider the relative success of these models in accounting for some relevant research findings.

Summary: what you have learned

In this chapter you have learned about what it takes to divide attention between several different things. You now know this is not always easy and that it can depend on things such as task similarity, task difficulty and practice. You have also learned how this applies to a specific real-word example: talking on a mobile phone while driving. Researchers have found that dividing attention through conversation makes driving performance worse, irrespective of whether the conversation is on a mobile phone, using a hands-free phone, or with someone in the car (e.g. Gugerty et al., 2004). However, it was noted that passengers in the car may stop conversations to allow the driver to pay attention.

You have learned that we can use selective attention to process one out of many different sensations. A key question for this area has been *when* the information is selected in our minds for additional processing. You have learned that there has been considerable debate around two approaches: an early selection approach and a late selection approach. You have also learned about an alternative to these models that is called load theory. You have learned that load theory proposes that we have a perceptual mechanism for selection and a cognitive mechanism for selection, and that the extent to which we ignore irrelevant distractions may depend upon the load of information on either mechanism.

You have also learned about visual spatial attention and what we know about its focus. You now know that early approaches used the analogies of a spotlight and a zoom lens, sharing the assumption that visual spatial attention has a single area of focus. You have learned that this view has changed in recent years, with researchers now suggesting that attention can be split across at least two different locations. It has been argued that these two viewpoints may simply represent two different ways that attention is focused, with a single focus acting as the 'default' option.

In this chapter you have also had an opportunity to develop your analysis and evaluation abilities through organising information to evaluate a claim about divided attention and driving. You have also had the opportunity to develop your decision-making skills by making judgements about some fictional evidence and whether it supports load theory.

Further reading

Johnson, A and Proctor, RW (2004) *Attention: theory and practice*. London: Sage Publications.

A broad textbook that provides a useful introduction to how the theoretical aspects of attention inform more practical matters such as the design of training or the display of information.

Lund, N (2012) *Attention (Foundations of Psychology)*. London: Routledge.

An up-to-date text that integrates evidence from cognitive psychology, neuropsychology and neuroscience.

Styles, EA (2006) *The psychology of attention*. 2nd edition. London: Psychology Press.

A popular book that provides a very accessible account, adding further depth to the broad areas covered here.

Chapter 7

Consciousness

Learning outcomes

By the end of this chapter you should:

- *be able to discuss what consciousness might mean and what it means for cognition;*

- *be able to describe some evidence of differences between* **conscious** *processes and* **unconscious** *processes;*

- *be able to analyse three different ways of measuring conscious awareness; and*

- *be able to reflect upon your own consciousness, as well as developing your organisational skills through evaluating a claim about research.*

Introduction

What does it mean to be conscious? What would life be like without consciousness? Can we determine if a mouse is conscious or not? Consciousness is generally regarded as a particularly difficult subject, and cognitive psychologists have often regarded these questions as something to be addressed by philosophers rather than with any systematic scientific investigation. Yet, this attitude is gradually changing and since the 1990s the subject of consciousness has attracted an increasing amount of attention. This attention has come not only from cognitive psychologists but also from researchers interested in the biological basis of psychology such as **neuroscientists** and **neurobiologists**. Consciousness has also received the continued attention of philosophers. Part of the challenge of consciousness is to determine which questions we can hope to possibly answer, and which ones we can't. In this chapter, we will start by considering some issues that are faced when trying to come up with a definition. For the remainder of the chapter we will consider what we can learn from the perspective of cognitive psychology. We will therefore be focusing on consciousness in terms of the scientific understanding of processes in the mind.

Defining consciousness

To understand what cognitive psychology can contribute to debates about consciousness, we must first learn a little about what some of those debates are. The first is working out how best to define consciousness.

Task ⎤ In your own words, try to define what consciousness means to you. You may want to consider what you mean if you say *I am conscious of that*, or what you understand if someone says that they were unconscious. Try to be as precise as possible.

William James (1890) suggested that one important property of consciousness is the idea that it is something that we experience in a continuous way – what he called the stream of consciousness. One of the clearest examples of this is blinking. Although we blink regularly we do not experience a break in consciousness every time we blink. Instead, we experience the world as something consistent that exists all of the time.

According to Velmans (2009) the simplest place to start is how we use the term consciousness in everyday language. The starting point is therefore the simple presence or absence of experienced **phenomena**. If I do not experience something, I am not conscious of it. If I do experience it, then I am.

Interestingly, this feeling of consciousness consists of lots of different experiences that are specific to us. For example, I have no way of knowing if what I perceive as the 'blueness' of the cover of this book is the same as the 'blueness' that you experience. We have both learned a similar label (although you may be calling it 'turquoise'), but there is no independent way of knowing that we are having exactly the same experience. These experiences in our consciousness are therefore unique to each individual and are qualitative (we cannot express them precisely in quantities or numbers). The word that has been used to label these types of experience is the word *qualia*.

Critical thinking activity

What is it like to be a bat?

Critical thinking focus: reflection

Key question: *What does it mean to have consciousness?*

In this activity you will practise a skill known as reflection. Broadly speaking, reflection is when you think in depth about your experiences, actions, feelings and responses to them in a way that you might not usually do.

In this activity I want you to reflect upon what it means to you to be conscious, and we will use a simple question to get you started: what is it like to be a bat? This question was posed formally by the philosopher Nagel (1974), and is an interesting question to consider. While reflecting on this, try to consider some or all of the following issues.

– Does a bat experience feeling in its toes?

– Does a bat get an itch?

Does a bat think about tomorrow?

Does a bat have consciousness like you have consciousness?

How would we ever know?

Continue to reflect about what it might mean to be conscious beyond these few questions. Ask yourself why you believe what you believe, and challenge yourself on the assumptions you make. Ask yourself whether it is definitely true. Importantly, consider if there is any way you can definitely know.

Critical thinking review

This activity helps to develop your reflection skills while thinking about the nature of consciousness. In particular, this activity gives you an opportunity to step back and notice the assumptions you might make about the consciousness of others. For example, you may discover beliefs you never realised you had. You may notice that your feelings may affect how you think about things. For example, is it important to you that a bat has a different type of consciousness to you? Being able to take a step back and look at experiences from a distance helps you identify the assumptions or biases you may have, and how they may be clouding your thinking.

In terms of what it is like to be a bat, well, I have no idea, and I would never claim to. This is important because, for everyone, there is a part of being conscious that is entirely personal that no one can ever know. You may disagree, but despite our strongest-held beliefs, it is unlikely that we will ever know if a bat experiences consciousness in the same way as we do personally. It may be exactly the same. It may be completely different. Or it may be somewhere in-between. Understanding those things we may never know, through careful reflection, is an important skill to develop.

Other skills you may have used in this activity include: analysing and evaluating; and comparison.

According to Block (1995) we have to be careful to be very specific about what we refer to when we use the word consciousness. Block (1995) argues that we can distinguish between at least two different types of consciousness: access consciousness and phenomenal consciousness. Phenomenal consciousness consists of those subjective experiences and feelings in consciousness (such as the blueness of the blue of the cover to this book). These are not under our direct control, but we experience them as something that we are conscious of. In contrast, access consciousness refers to consciousness that interacts with our cognitive processes and is used for tasks such as reasoning and speech. This is when we feel we have direct conscious control over our thoughts and actions.

From the description of access consciousness it should be clear that this type of consciousness fits into the type that cognitive psychologists have the research tools and experience to study. One thing cognitive psychologists can add to the debate on consciousness is information on how consciousness relates to other areas of cognition such as thinking and decision making, learning and memory, perception and attention.

For the rest of this chapter we will therefore focus on studies that tell us something about the relationships between cognitive processes and consciousness. We will explore whether conscious awareness is always required for cognitive processing, or whether some processing can occur in the absence of consciousness. More specifically, we will ask if we can unconsciously learn something, or if our behaviours can be influenced by things we claim not to be able to experience.

Importantly, we won't address the question of why we experience *qualia* in the way that we do, whether the mind is separate from the body, or whether a bat can have consciousness. Some authors refer to these types of question as the 'hard problem' (e.g. Chalmers, 1996), and it is enough to note that there are no easy answers. Instead, we will focus upon the way in which consciousness may relate to the processes of the mind. The first of these that you will learn about is the relationship between consciousness and the implicit learning of grammar.

Unconscious grammar

In Chapter 4, on language, you learned that grammar is important when we think about how we use and understand language. You will probably have spent many of your early years in school learning about grammar in simple sentences – for example, what a noun is, how to use a verb and where these go in sentences in English. When you learn about grammar in this way you are conscious of what you're learning and have clear and explicit awareness of trying to remember the rules and using them in sentences. One interesting suggestion is that some grammar can be learned at a level that you don't have this strong conscious awareness of. In other words, while you can learn the rules of grammar explicitly (such as in school), grammar is also supported through learning that occurs implicitly outside conscious awareness.

Task — On a piece of paper, try to write down everything you know about English grammar. Pay particular attention to whether there is anything that you feel that you would 'know it if I saw it' but can't put into words.

It is worth noting here that the terms *experience*, *awareness* and *conscious awareness* are often used to refer to the same idea. While there may be subtle differences between these terms, when you first begin to think about consciousness it is enough to be aware that these terms are referring to broadly the same idea (Velmans, 2009).

While the amount of research on consciousness has grown recently, it was back in 1967 when Reber first demonstrated that participants were able to learn an artificial grammar without conscious awareness of doing so. The grammar was referred to as an artificial grammar because it was made up for the purposes of the experiments. More specifically, the participants in Reber's (1967) first experiment were not told that they were learning a grammar; instead, they were told that they were taking part in a simple memory experiment. Participants were briefly shown sets of letter strings (for five seconds each) and then required to write down as many of these strings as they could remember correctly. Examples of the letter strings are TPPTS and VXVPS. The experimenter gave them feedback on which ones they got right and which ones they got wrong. The same sets were then repeated until participants correctly remembered all of them. This procedure was repeated seven times in total, with seven different sets of letter strings. Reber (1967) looked at how quickly, and how accurately, participants learned these strings.

The important aspect of this experiment was that Reber (1967) treated two different groups of participants in two different ways. The first group were shown letter strings that were completely random and had no underlying relationship with each other. In contrast, the second group were shown letter strings based on a grammar that he had made up. In Figure 7.1 you can see the diagram that Reber (1967) used to explain the structure of his artificial grammar. We can use this diagram to produce letter strings that are 'grammatical' according to this artificial grammar. Starting from the left we can see that TPPTS is allowed (or even TPPPTS or TPPPPPTS). However, it is not possible to have VPTXV.

The question that Reber (1967) asked was whether participants would learn the grammar through simply being exposed to the strings. In other words, would participants learn this grammar although they are unaware that they were doing so? For the first two sets of letter strings it was found that there were no real differences. It did not matter whether there were hidden

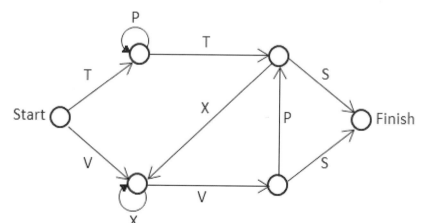

Figure 7.1:
Schematic diagram of the artificial grammar used by Reber (1967)

grammatical rules or not; participants were making the same number of errors. However, from the third set onwards it was found that participants were making significantly fewer errors if they were in the group that was viewing the letter strings that had the underlying grammar. Although unaware of it, participants were learning something that made them better at the task of remembering these sets. This result is particularly interesting because participants believed they were taking part in a memory experiment and they had not been made aware of the presence (or absence) of an underlying grammatical structure.

In a second experiment, Reber (1967) added an additional testing phase to the above procedure. In this testing phase he told participants that what they had learned followed some 'grammatical rules'. They were then shown more letter strings and were asked to identify which they thought were grammatical and which they thought were non-grammatical. You might find yourself making similar judgements if you say something and then think that it doesn't 'sound right'. You know it doesn't fit the grammatical rules but can't explicitly say why. In this version of the experiment it was found that participants were able to correctly identify the grammatical strings more often than you would expect by chance. This confirmed the idea that they had indeed learned the artificial grammar to some extent. Thinking about consciousness, the important question becomes whether this was learned with no awareness of the grammar.

Task — In your own words, describe the task used by Reber (1967). Use his diagram to create examples of letter strings that would be grammatical and some examples of letter strings that would not be grammatical. Explain in your own words what the results tell us about consciousness.

Dienes and Scott (2005) have since distinguished between structural knowledge and judgement knowledge in implicit learning tasks similar to those of Reber (1967). An example of structural knowledge would be the knowledge that a string can start with the letter 'T' or usually ends with an 'S'. When this is used to make a judgement, such as deciding if a sentence is grammatical, then that becomes a piece of judgement knowledge. The importance of highlighting this difference is that it is only the structural knowledge that is unconscious; the judgement knowledge is conscious. In implicit learning tasks, such as those described above, participants can make judgements better than chance because they are conscious that a letter string does not meet the appropriate rules (it 'sounds right' or 'feels wrong'), although they are not necessarily conscious of what those rules are (Destrebecqz and Cleeremans, 2001).

Criteria for consciousness

One limitation of research on the sort of implicit learning described above has been highlighted by Shanks and St John (1994). They observed that the distinction between explicit and implicit knowledge may not explain the results entirely. Instead, they suggested that participants may be completing the tasks using instances rather than rules. For instance, they might be remembering seeing a word that looked similar to the one that they are judging to be grammatical. Importantly, participants may be consciously aware of these instances although they are not conscious of the 'rule'. This is important because what might be a fairly conscious process – making judgements based on instances – is being described as if it is an unconscious process.

Shanks and St John (1994) proposed two criteria that should be applied when deciding if behaviour is truly influenced by unconscious learning: the information criterion and the sensitivity criterion.

The information criterion suggests that before we decide that our participants are not aware of what they have learned that is changing their behaviour, we have to make sure that what we are looking for in the awareness test is what is influencing the behaviour. To apply this to the example we are working with, the experimenter checks to see if the participant is aware of the 'rules' because we might believe that this is what is influencing their behaviour. This does not meet the criterion because it may not be 'rules' that are influencing the behaviour but 'instances' instead. We should therefore be checking whether the participant is aware of the instances, as well as whether they are aware of the rules.

The second criterion is the sensitivity criterion. The sensitivity criterion suggests that to demonstrate that our two measures of awareness and task performance actually relate to two different cognitive processes, we have to be able to demonstrate that our measure is sensitive to all possible levels of relevant conscious knowledge. To apply this to our example, asking if people are aware of the rules is not particularly sensitive. For example, it is easy to imagine that people may say they are not aware of any rules, but if you give them some examples, they may point out that they knew they all ended in 'S' and only started with either a 'T' or a 'V'.

These criteria are important, because in looking at conscious awareness, or a lack of it, we must be able to defend the idea that something is happening that is truly unconscious. If what we are measuring may not be actually influencing the behaviour, or our measure doesn't test all possible levels of conscious knowledge, then it becomes harder to defend the idea that this is truly the case.

Measuring awareness

In the previous section you have learned about research findings in which it is assumed that the participants are not consciously aware of the mental processes involved. For example, participants are not aware that they have learned a form of grammar. We find this research interesting because the individuals' behaviour has changed and is influenced by these experiences even if they are not aware of it.

An important aspect of scientific research is to be clear about the assumptions that you are making. You have already learned that a significant challenge for researchers interested in levels of consciousness is the extent to which participants are actually conscious of processes. The 'level' of consciousness of any experience is not easy to define, but many researchers believe there must be more than two levels – in other words, there must be more than being either conscious or unconscious. This poses a challenge because a researcher would ideally need to know 'how' conscious the participant in the experiment is of their own mental processes. We mentioned this when you learned about the sensitivity criterion. You also learned that we may never truly know someone else's conscious experience. We must therefore rely upon a participant's report of how aware they are.

A participant reporting on their experience is known as a **subjective measure** because it relies upon the person being studied to report it to the researcher. The opposite of this is an **objective measure**; this would be something that someone could independently measure. Physical properties such as height or eye colour are examples of things that can be objectively measured; you do not have to rely on what that person says their height or eye colour is – you can measure it for yourself. Unfortunately, awareness and consciousness cannot be directly measured, and we must rely upon what the person says. It is therefore important to think about how we can get our participants to report their experiences as accurately as possible. A few specific measures have been developed, three of which are:

- confidence ratings;

- the perceptual awareness scale;

- post-decision wagering.

Confidence ratings

Confidence ratings have generally been used when investigating unconscious perception (e.g. Bernstein and Eriksen, 1965). These ratings require participants to rate how confident they are with a decision, such as how confident they are that they saw something (Bernstein and Eriksen, 1965; Cheesman and Merikle, 1986). Alternatively, participants may rate how confident they are that they have provided a correct answer to a question or to any other response they have made (e.g. Dienes et al., 1995).

An advantage of collecting the data like this is that the judgement can be made straight after a participant has seen or done something, rather than at a later point. However, a clear disadvantage is that people may have different criteria for deciding if they are confident or not. That is to say, two people may have the same clarity of awareness in their conscious experience, but one of them may have a bias towards rating themselves as having low confidence while the other may have a bias towards reporting high confidence, despite both having the same clarity of experience (Sandberg et al., 2010). One alternative would be to ask participants to rate the clarity of their experience more directly.

The perceptual awareness scale

Interestingly, one problem with many scales is that they may not be related to how participants are experiencing the task. For example, you will most likely have some experience of filling in questionnaires or surveys. You may have completed one when asked by someone in the street, you may have been sent one by post or e-mail, or you may even have filled one in at your doctor's or dentist's surgery. One thing the questionnaire may have asked you to do was to rate something on a scale. For example you may have been asked to rate how much you enjoyed something on a scale from 1 to 10 with 10 indicating that you greatly enjoyed it and 1 indicating that you didn't enjoy it at all. People can sometimes get frustrated by filling these in, as they may not believe that the scale has all the options they want, or they become unsure which number refers to their experience if given little indication what each specific number means. This is a particularly important issue when researching something like consciousness, but any scale must clearly, reliably and accurately represent that person's experience. The solution that Ramsøy and Overgaard (2004) used when developing the perceptual awareness scale (PAS) was to get their participants to develop the scale instead.

Task ——— Imagine you had to rate how clearly you find things in your day-to-day conscious experiences. One scale would be just to have 'conscious' as the first option and 'unconscious' at the second option. Try to design a scale with at least four options that you think would capture all of your experiences.

Participants in Ramsøy and Overgaard's (2004) experiment viewed visual displays that were shown very briefly. They were then asked to describe the quality of their visual experience using a scale they created themselves. The researchers gave some initial suggestions, but it was left to the individual participants to decide what it should look like. From the scales that their participants produced, the researchers developed the following: (1) No experience; (2) Brief glimpse; (3) Almost clear image; and (4) Absolutely clear image.

This scale has the advantage that it is perhaps more intuitive and easy to understand than something such as a confidence rating. Part of the reason for this may be that it relies upon natural distinctions that mean more to the participants, rather than forcing the participants to use categories that may seem artificial.

It has been argued that a disadvantage of scales is that they rely upon participants accurately and happily disclosing information. Some participants may not be willing to admit they are not confident, or not aware, of something and instead withhold information because they have no motivation to reveal it (Persaud et al., 2007). A potential alternative that does not have this problem is post-decision wagering.

Post-decision wagering

Post-decision wagering is when a participant is required to place a bet, with money, on how accurate their decisions are (e.g. Persaud et al., 2007; Persaud and McLeod, 2008). Participants are required to decide whether they wish to place a low wager or a high wager on one of two possibilities.

For example, Persaud and McLeod (2008) briefly presented either the letter 'b' or the letter 'h' to their participants. Participants had to say the letter that was not shown. So if the letter 'b' was flashed up they would have to say 'h'. Participants also had to bet on whether they were correct. They had the option of betting a small amount of money (low wager) or a larger amount of money (high wager).

The logic behind this is that participants will bet according to their awareness. This does not explicitly require them to report their awareness, such as on a scale, but merely asks them to act upon it. This means that problems such as having to pick a number that reflects a personal experience are avoided. The potential to gain money from the wager also means that participants are more motivated to act according to their actual awareness.

In the example from Persaud and McLeod (2008) participants were betting on the letter they thought they saw. Participants were more likely to bet the higher amount when they had seen the letter for a relatively long time (15 ms) compared to very briefly (5–10 ms). Interestingly, when seen briefly, participants were reluctant to bet a large amount even when they were generally correct. This is interesting because the fact they are generally correct suggests there was some processing of the information, but their reluctance to place a high bet suggests they are not completely consciously aware of it.

While this approach is novel, and appears not to have some of the other limitations, it remains to be seen if this is a more reliable measure of conscious awareness. Indeed, while it claims to measure consciousness more directly, it may be limited by the criteria that an individual uses to wager (Clifford et al., 2008). That is to say, two individuals may have similar conscious experiences, but one of them may be more inclined to place high wagers whenever they can, while the other may only place high wagers when their experience is completely clear (e.g. Dienes and Seth, 2010).

Task ⌐ Explain, in your own words, what post-decision wagering involves. Describe any advantages or disadvantages you can think of with this approach.

Measuring awareness is not straightforward yet the three approaches presented here represent an interesting starting point. The central difficulty of each of these measures is that they all rely upon the person taking part to do something that indicates their level of awareness. This introduces difficulties because of differences between people in how they judge their own awareness, how they judge their own confidence, and how they decide when to place a high or low wager.

Blindsight

In the next chapter of this book you will learn about cognitive neuropsychology. Cognitive neuropsychology is when we study individuals who have had a brain injury or illness that has affected their normal cognitive processes. Up until this point we have focused on what we can learn about cognition from healthy participants; in contrast, cognitive neuropsychology can reveal something about cognition by looking at what happens with patients who have had injuries and illnesses. Although we have saved this until last, the investigation of one particular condition, called blindsight, has important implications for our thoughts on consciousness and will be discussed here.

In very simple terms, blindsight is when a person reports having no awareness of vision in a specific part of their visual field yet they are able to complete visual tasks for information in these same areas, such as pointing at targets or identifying them from two choices. Importantly, they perform these tasks correctly at levels above chance despite their reported lack of any conscious awareness. This type of phenomena is usually associated with a lesion in the area of their brain that is called the primary visual cortex. While cases were originally highlighted by Riddoch (1917) as well as Pöppel et al. (1973), perhaps the most intensively studied case was first reported by Weiskrantz et al. (1974) when they documented a series of experiments with a patient known as DB.

Weiskrantz et al. (1974) reported how DB did not have any conscious awareness of anything in the lower-left quadrant of his visual field. This was the result of a surgical procedure that removed a deformity on his brain at the age of 26. Nevertheless, when asked to reach for targets in this part of his visual field DB was found to perform at levels above chance. Importantly, this occurred despite him having no conscious visual experience of seeing anything in this part of his visual field. Similar results were found when asked to discriminate between the presence of an 'X' or an 'O', and when discriminating between vertical and horizontal lines.

Further studies with other people with blindsight have revealed similar results. This has included demonstrating above-chance performance for cognitive processes such as the processing of colour information (e.g. Stoerig and Cowey, 1992), the processing of emotion in expressions (e.g. de Gelder et al., 1999) and even the processing of the meanings of words (e.g. Marcel, 1998). Interestingly, there have also been indications that someone with blindsight has the potential to perform better on some tasks in the 'blind' areas of their visual field compared to areas of normal vision (Trevethan et al., 2007).

Task ─┐ In your own words, describe what blindsight involves. Include information on how a
      │ typical blindsight patient might act and how they might report their experience.

So why is blindsight so important? Research into consciousness has another particular problem that is difficult to solve. You have learned already that an important aspect of cognitive psychology is the use of the scientific method. An important part of this method is that we vary something that we are manipulating (our independent variable) while we keep everything else as constant as possible. This is so that we know that any difference we observe is due to that one thing we have varied, and not due to anything else. This becomes challenging when we become interested in consciousness because we may be interested in the differences between conscious processing and unconscious processing.

Ideally, then, we need to find some way to manipulate consciousness (e.g. aware versus unaware) while keeping everything else constant. If we make someone 'unaware' of something, we may also have to alter the procedure to do this. For example, we may present something very fast. If we alter the procedure too much, then we do not know if anything we observe is due to the lack of consciousness or just due to the changes we have made. Ideally, we need to be able to manipulate the level of awareness without changing anything at all. To begin to solve this conundrum we would need someone who was both aware and unaware at the same time. Patients with blindsight are therefore particularly interesting because they make excellent candidates for this type of manipulation.

A particular issue in this area of research is, therefore, whether blindsight patients completely lack any awareness in the affected area. Indeed, there have been a number of alternative explanations put forward. One idea is that these patients may have 'islands' of information available to them that may explain above-chance performance in discrimination tasks (e.g. Campion et al., 1983; King et al., 1996). An important distinction is therefore between type one and type two blindsight (Weiskrantz, 1998). It has been suggested that type two blindsight has more conscious awareness and is characterised by having a 'feeling' in a way that type one is not.

Research in this area has also been criticised for relying on subjective patient reports of their own awareness. Why consciousness research has to rely on these reports was discussed earlier. A particular issue for blindsight research is that patients are often given only two choices in reporting their awareness: awareness and no awareness (Overgaard, 2011). Interestingly, Overgaard et al. (2008) tested a blindsight patient and recorded her awareness using the PAS instead. You have learned already that the PAS is a scale with four points on it: (1) No experience; (2) Brief glimpse; (3) Almost clear image; and (4) Absolutely clear image. When tested in this way her above-chance performance corresponded to some level of awareness, albeit a 'brief glimpse', and above-chance performance was no longer associated with 'no experience'. It is suggested by these researchers that one of the most important aspects of blindsight, that of above-chance task performance in the complete absence of awareness, may therefore be a result of the testing procedures. This interpretation is currently controversial but is an important consideration to make when learning about this fascinating phenomenon.

Skill builder activity

Now you see it, now you don't

Transferable skill focus: organisational skills

Key question: *How are people with blindsight asked to report their conscious awareness?*

You have learned about blindsight, a condition in which people claim to be unable to see in an area of their visual field but perform above-chance on tasks that make use of information in it. You have also learned of one potential criticism, that people with blindsight may be indicating their awareness with only two limited options, aware and unaware (see Overgaard et al., 2008). With this activity we will make use of the internet to organise information so we can make a judgement on the extent to which this is true.

On a computer open up an internet browser (such as Internet Explorer, Firefox or Google Chrome) and navigate to a suitable search tool (such as www.google.co.uk or www.bing.co.uk). From here we are going to find a database of research abstracts to use. A research abstract is a short summary of a piece of research that tells you what the problem was that was being researched, what the researchers did, what they found, and what they think it means. It is possible to find databases of research abstracts that are just from psychological research. One well-known database is PsycINFO® but you may need to pay to use it. If you are currently studying at university or college, then where you are studying may already be paying for you to have access and it is worth checking with them to see if you can use it. There are currently freely available databases such as PubMED that are not specific to just psychological research but are more helpful than a general search of the whole internet. If you do not have access to PsycINFO®, then use a search tool to find the website for PubMED.

Now that you are on a website that provides a database of research abstracts, use the search facility to look for 'Blindsight'. A relatively long list of titles of research will be displayed. You may or may not have to click on the title to be able to read the whole abstract depending on the database you are using. Read the abstract and try to determine if the person with blindsight indicated their awareness on a two-point scale or in a way that has more options. You may find it useful to also look in the methods section of the paper if you have access.

Create a table and make a note of what you find. You may find it useful to have columns that allow you to indicate if they used a two-point scale or not (perhaps 'two-point? Yes/No/Unclear') as well as columns to record the names of the authors, the year, and the title of the article. Repeat this exercise for four or five abstracts/articles (or as many as you like). You should be able to see that being organised in this way helps you to make judgements about claims that have been made. In an ideal world you would find every possible article so that you can make a clear unbiased judgement (this is sometimes known as a systematic review). For the purposes of developing your skills, four or five should be sufficient. When you have finished, use the information you have gathered and organised in your table to judge if most studies used a two-point scale.

Skill builder review

This activity helps develop your organisational skills, focusing on your ability to search for and organise information that is available in scientific literature. This is important because it allows you to have a clearly structured overview of the knowledge that exists. Being organised with this also makes sure you do not use the same articles twice, and helps you identify gaps that you might need to fill with further research.

Other skills you may have used in this activity: information technology; decision making; and independent learning.

Assignments

1. Defend the idea that the learning of artificial grammar can be implicit. Outline evidence that suggests implicit learning of grammar occurs and highlight potential limitations with this conclusion. Present these so that you can defend the idea that implicit learning exists.

2. Evaluate three different measures of conscious awareness. Describe, with examples, how each works and the types of responses that are usually collected. Explain the strengths of each approach, and discuss any weaknesses.

3. Describe the phenomenon of blindsight and explain what we can conclude about consciousness from them. State the basic ideas behind the condition, and consider any strengths or weaknesses and how they might limit any explanations.

Summary: what you have learned

You have learned that consciousness can be hard to define and even more difficult to measure. To help us focus on the 'easy' problems you have learned about access consciousness and what we can learn from studies about how consciousness is related to cognition.

You have learned that some studies have shown that artificial grammars may be learned by simply being exposed to letter sequences that have an implicit grammatical structure. You know now that there may be a distinction between judgement knowledge (that is conscious) and structural knowledge (that is unconscious). You have also found out about criteria that need to be considered whenever implicit learning is claimed: the information criterion and the sensitivity criterion.

You are now aware of some of the particular difficulties of researching consciousness, particularly the challenges of measuring someone's conscious awareness. You now know about three measures that some researchers have chosen to use: confidence ratings; the perceptual awareness scale; and post-decision wagering.

You have also learned about the curious case of blindsight, where people claim not to be able to see something but can do better than chance on different tasks. You now know that this is important because we are able to look at both conscious awareness and a lack of awareness with the same participant in the same task with few changes to it. This helps us closely study the differences between cognitive processes with and without consciousness.

Throughout this chapter you have had an opportunity to develop your reflective skills through carefully considering what it means to be conscious. You have also had the opportunity to develop your organisational skills by critically evaluating one claim about research with blindsight patients.

Further reading

Blackmore, S (2010) *Consciousness: an introduction*. 2nd edition. London: Hodder Education.

An important student text that provides a much broader coverage of topics in consciousness research, including neuroscience and altered states of consciousness.

Torey, Z (2009) *The crucible of consciousness: an integrated theory of mind and brain*. London: MIT Press.

An interesting text that outlines a clear hypothesis on how consciousness may be related to more specific brain functioning.

Velmans, M (2009) *Understanding consciousness*. 2nd edition. London: Routledge.

An excellent and highly accessible book that draws together the philosophical aspects of consciousness with scientific advances.

Chapter 8

Cognitive neuropsychology

Learning outcomes

By the end of this chapter you should:

- *be able to discuss the characteristics that define cognitive neuropsychology;*

- *be able to describe how patient HM has developed our understanding of memory;*

- *be able to analyse how patient KF has helped develop our understanding of perception; and*

- *be able to think critically and creatively about how to test for specific deficits, as well as developing your teamwork through research.*

Introduction

Other chapters in this book have been introduced by showing how we use cognitive processes on a daily basis: from solving problems to recognising that something is far away or paying attention to relevant information. Cognitive neuropsychology is different from those other topics such as reasoning, perception and attention. Instead of being a subject area formed around a type of cognitive process, it is a division of cognitive psychology that is characterised by the type of information it uses to challenge theories. Those theories could come from any of the subject areas you have learned about already (reasoning, attention etc.). So unless you are a patient with a head injury or other damage to your brain, this chapter does not apply to you on a daily basis. It does, however, provide some fascinating insights into how we can clarify how the mind works.

As we start, it is important to note that we must be very careful when we think about cognitive neuropsychology. Indeed, we will spend the first part of this chapter thinking carefully about what it is, what it isn't, what it assumes and how the data are collected. This is important because when you understand these aspects, then you will be able to think clearly about what the data mean, and what can be learned from studying patients.

In the second half of this chapter you will learn about examples from cognitive neuropsychology that inform our thinking. We will focus on concepts that you are already familiar with if you have read the previous chapters in this book. Specifically, you will learn about patients with impaired memories and patients with impaired visual processing. You will learn about some of the symptoms of these patients and it will be shown how these can help us put together better cognitive theories. To start, we must first understand what cognitive neuropsychology is.

Defining cognitive neuropsychology

In Chapter 7 (on consciousness) you learned that cognitive neuropsychology is the study of individuals with a brain injury or illness that has affected their normal cognitive processes. You may be familiar with some of the terms used for groups of patients with similar symptoms. For example, you may have heard of amnesia (memory impairments) or aphasia (language impairments). You may have even heard about prosopagnosia, an impairment in recognising faces. Each of these is known as a syndrome. While all these patients can be labelled as having a syndrome, they will share some common symptoms only; each individual patient will also have their differences and uniqueness.

People working in a clinical setting (doctors, nurses, therapists etc.) may find these labels useful for their job of diagnosis or treatment. In contrast, a cognitive neuropsychologist is less interested in them. This is because cognitive neuropsychology is mainly concerned with studying the symptoms of each patient. These symptoms are studied to work out the cause of the cognitive problem, and to learn what it tells us about normal cognition. An understanding of the symptoms of a patient are then used to support or challenge cognitive theories about unimpaired processing. For example, later on you will learn about how the symptoms of a patient called HM have taught us about normal functioning memory.

Task — In your own words, outline what it is that cognitive neuropsychologists study.

So cognitive neuropsychology is most often about studying symptoms, and is not about studying syndromes in general. Another important thing to note is that a cognitive neuropsychologist is not usually interested in what part of the brain is damaged. What I mean by this is that a cognitive neuropsychologist is unlikely to be interested in explaining which parts of the brain are responsible for different things. This is not to say that the part of the brain involved is not important; in fact, it is a useful indicator as to the type of symptoms a patient may have. However, whether a certain area of the brain is associated with a particular cognitive process is a side-issue. Some studies may address it, and it is, of course, interesting, but it is not necessarily the main aim of an investigation. The main aim is to understand the patients' symptoms in terms of damage to cognitive systems and processes. This information can then be used to develop our understanding of normal cognitive processes and systems in the mind. If this is clear, then an important question now is: what methods are used to achieve this?

Methods and assumptions

You have learned already that cognitive neuropsychology uses data from patients with brain damage to learn something about unimpaired processing of information in the mind, as well as explaining the symptoms. To do this there are some assumptions that must be made and methods that may be used. For cognitive neuropsychology to 'make sense' these assumptions are important over and above those we would normally have in cognitive psychology. This section of the chapter will look at some of the main assumptions, including:

* universality;

* modularity;

* transparency;

* subtractivity.

Once you have learned about these assumptions you will learn about two other important aspects of the methods generally used: double dissociations and single-case studies. While these methods and assumptions are the most widely used, they are not the only ones.

Main assumptions

Universality

The first assumption is a straightforward one. We are going to look at the cognitive processes of a few patients and use it to help us develop our theories of cognition, as well as understanding where their processes have gone wrong. We must therefore assume that the way the mind is organised is generally the same for everyone. This is known as the assumption of universality (Caramazza, 1986). This is important because if we don't assume it, then we can learn much less about our minds from looking at those of others. Indeed, we need to continue to make further assumptions about the organisation of the mind. The next important assumption is that our minds are actually **modular**.

Modularity

Modularity is an assumption about how the mind is organised. It is assumed that the mind consists of separate components. Each component makes an individual contribution to the overall system. That is to say, if you remove a component, the overall system still works, but in a slightly different way. One way of looking at this idea of modularity was proposed by Fodor (1983). This is known more generally as Fodorian modularity.

Fodor (1983) proposed many different properties a cognitive **module** must have. As this is a brief introduction to this area, there is not enough space to learn about each of these in depth. However, it is worth noting the ideas that modules require informational encapsulation and should be **domain-specific**. Let's deal with each of these in turn.

Informational encapsulation, as put forward by Fodor (1983), is the idea that each module operates in such a way that it does not need to 'find out' anything from any other module. That is to say, the processes in that module are independent of processes in other modules.

A domain-specific module is one that deals only with one type of input. For example, a module might process visual information (such as shape, size or colour) but not process its position in space. The module is specific to a 'domain' of information.

Now, if we assume that cognition is modular in structure, then we also need to make assumptions about what happens when you damage one of these modules.

Transparency

The idea of transparency (Caramazza, 1984) builds upon the assumption of modularity. It is assumed that looking at impairments will give us some idea about the modules that have been impaired. In other words, we have to assume that if you remove a module, the structure of the overall system does not change. That is to say, removing a module (damaging a cognitive component) does not lead to new parts in the system, whether they be components or processes. If this was the case, then studying the impairments would tell us nothing about the systems underneath it; they would not be transparent to us and our studying of them. A closely related issue is that of subtractivity.

Subtractivity

Following brain damage, some patients are known to find novel ways of using their cognitive systems to complete tasks. For example, patients who have trouble processing spoken words are known to pay greater attention to the lips to try to make sense of what they are hearing (e.g. Albert and Bear, 1974). Even though this happens, it is assumed that it does not make use of any new components. Instead, it is assumed that the patient is making novel use of existing ones. This general idea has been referred to as 'subtractivity' (e.g. Saffran, 1982; Coltheart, 2001): the brain damage is assumed to subtract something from the overall system. Importantly, it is assumed that the damage cannot add anything. This is important because it helps us interpret patterns of impairments in terms of what is missing from the underlying cognitive components. This interpretation is further helped by what we call dissociations and, more importantly, double dissociations.

Double dissociations

Double dissociations are not just important when it comes to cognitive neuropsychology. They can also be used when thinking about experiments with other participants. To understand the principles of a double dissociation we will start with a single dissociation.

Up to this point you may have the idea that all we care about is what someone has wrong with their cognitive processes (impairments). While this is important, it is the *pattern* of impairments compared to what has been spared that is most important. So it is not just what is lost but what is still there that is informative. This is best illustrated with an example.

It is worth noting that while this example uses fictional patients, the impairments are based upon actual case studies (see Patterson and Marcel, 1977; Warrington, 1981). Imagine we have a patient called MJ. MJ is very good at reading words that are concrete. MJ has no trouble reading out word lists such as *house, frog, tent, fridge* and *library*. Yet if you ask MJ to read out a list of abstract words, he has some trouble. For example, it is unlikely that he will be able to read many of the words on this list: *hope, fear, truth, freedom* and *liberty*. As strange as it sounds, the symptoms of MJ are selective impairments for the reading of abstract words. On this basis alone, can we conclude that concrete words and abstract words might require different cognitive modules?

We may feel that this is good evidence, but it is only a single dissociation. A simple explanation may be that the tasks differ in how hard or easy they are. That is to say, after any brain damage, reading abstract words may be harder than reading concrete words. For example, concrete words may be more familiar to MJ, or MJ may have learned them at an earlier age. Perhaps, all we can conclude is that after the brain damage MJ is not very good at difficult reading tasks. This isn't quite as exciting or quite as interesting. This data would be more useful if we had a patient with the opposite problem. Let's call her CM.

CM isn't very good at reading concrete words. Unlike MJ, she performs perfectly well when asked to read out lists of abstract words, such as *hope, fear, truth, freedom* and *liberty*. However, she doesn't do very well at all when reading out lists of concrete words such as *house, frog, tent, fridge* and *library*. If we look at CM together with MJ, we can come to some more exciting conclusions because they form a *double dissociation*. What MJ is good at CM is not so good at, and what CM is good at MJ is not so good at. This is a double dissociation and it supports the idea that reading concrete words and reading abstract words might require two different modules. We can claim that this idea is supported because our two patients demonstrate that the two abilities can be damaged independently of each other. We might not find this pattern with these patients if they were exactly the same module.

If we want to think about double dissociations in more general terms, we might put it in the following way: Patient A demonstrates impaired performance in Task 1 but unimpaired performance in Task 2, while Patient B demonstrates impaired performance in Task 2 but unimpaired performance in Task 1.

This pattern of impairment and sparing in a double dissociation provides a much stronger argument when developing theories (e.g. Teuber, 1955; Shallice, 1979). This is not to say that all developments in this area rely upon these double dissociations. They do, however, provide some of the most convincing evidence and are therefore an important method.

Task ⌐ Draw a diagram that illustrates the idea of double dissociations. Feel free to be creative but make sure that it clearly demonstrates your thoughts.

While the interpretation of double dissociations is on the surface straightforward, it has been questioned repeatedly over the course of cognitive neuropsychology's development (e.g. Juola and Plunkett, 2000). The exact nature of these criticisms is not important at this stage, and neither are the numerous defences. Instead, it is simply worth noting that double dissociations have remained the 'gold standard' in cognitive neuropsychology.

Of course, establishing these sorts of patterns is only the beginning. It is necessary that further investigations are conducted. These investigations are needed to work out the details of the individual processes/systems that are spared, and those that are impaired, if the data are going to be meaningful (Seidenberg, 1988).

It is also worth noting that this interpretation assumes everyone shares a similar set of modules. You have already learned that this assumption is known as universality. This assumption is important because we are often considering data from a single person. These are known as single-case studies, and this area relies upon them to a relatively large extent. But why is this?

Single-case studies

When we look at some examples later on you will learn about one or two individual patients. Convention in the research literature is to refer to them by their initials (such as DF or PW). This is a very different approach to collecting data about cognitive processes than you may be used to. In the other chapters you have learned about experiments that test larger groups of people, and come to conclusions about averages across or within these groups. One reason we do this is that people naturally vary. By testing more than one person we can get a measure of how much variability there is. We then use this to help us decide if the experiment shows something. In terms of studying patients this is a less useful approach (see Caramazza and McCloskey, 1988).

As noted above, cognitive neuropsychology is the study of symptoms to construct explanations based on cognitive processes. As no two patients present with exactly the same symptoms, or exactly the same brain damage, it is argued that group studies become inappropriate (e.g. Shallice, 1979; Ellis and Young, 1988). Nevertheless, some psychologists have reservations about single-case studies. They prefer to look at a 'series' of case studies in which several individuals with similar, but not identical, symptoms are studied in very similar ways (e.g. Patterson et al., 2006). Even in this case we might have to be very careful, as the symptoms may still not occur for the same reasons.

This leads us to a second and more practical point: patients with theoretically interesting symptoms are relatively rare and not necessarily easy to access. Similarly, even if they can be identified, patients may not always agree to take part in what can be a time-consuming process. In comparison to participants in other experiments mentioned in this book, patients often undergo long periods of intensive testing.

A participant in an attention experiment, such as those mentioned in Chapter 6, may undergo only one test and be tested for roughly 20 to 30 minutes. By comparison, a patient will be asked by cognitive neuropsychologists to take part in multiple tests on top of those that may have already been administered by the hospital. Some will be standardised tests that are used generally for diagnosis; others may be more specifically designed for their symptoms. Finally, other tests may be created especially for that patient. These non-standardised tests are developed for more in-depth investigation. These will build upon the results of previous tests where they indicate areas for further investigation. Testing can therefore take weeks, months or even be spread across a lifetime.

Task ⌐ In 500 words, outline why cognitive neuropsychology makes use of single-case studies more than other areas of cognitive psychology.

Now you have learned about the basics of what cognitive neuropsychology is, let's think about some specific patients and what we can learn from them. We'll start with patient HM, the study of whom has helped develop theories about human memory.

Impaired memory

You have already learned that cognitive neuropsychology tends to move forward by looking at specific symptoms in patients with brain damage. This information is then used both to identify a cause in terms of cognitive processes and to develop theories of the unimpaired mind. In this section you will learn about one specific case study, that of HM.

HM

The case of HM was first reported in the literature by Scoville and Milner (1957), and then in more detail latterly by Milner (1966). They described the case of a man who suffered from frequent epileptic seizures. His condition was not responding to the maximum amounts of medication, so a decision was taken to operate on his brain. This operation was highly experimental at the time and deliberately damaged areas in the brain. It was hoped the result of the damage would be to reduce the number and severity of the seizures. The exact location of the damaged areas is unimportant for our purposes. It is, however, noteworthy that we now believe that one of the areas in the brain that was damaged, the hippocampus, is a very important area for memory.

The general effects of this surgery were clear. In terms of his seizures, things were much better and he had a small number of seizures in subsequent years. However, an unexpected result was that HM had difficulty remembering all events after, and leading up to, the surgery. For example, he did not recognise the hospital staff or know where the toilets in the hospital were. Yet HM also found it fairly easy to remember events that happened over 20 months before the surgery. The effect of this is best illustrated with an example.

> Ten months ago the family moved from their old house to a new one a few blocks away on the same street; he still has not learned the new address, though remembering the old one perfectly, nor can he be trusted to find his way home alone. Moreover, he does not know where objects in continual use are kept; for example, his mother still has to tell him where to find the lawn mower, even though he may have been using it only the day before . . . Yet to a casual observer this man seems like a relatively normal individual, since his understanding and reasoning are undiminished.
>
> (Scoville and Milner, 1957: 25–26)

HM clearly had difficulty in learning new information and updating what he knew about the world. This applied from the point of having surgery, and slightly before. Problems of forming new memories are known as anterograde amnesia. HM shares these symptoms with many other amnesics.

In contrast, HM had relatively intact memories from his life before surgery. If HM had impaired memory for his early life, then we would have called this retrograde amnesia. While it is not the case with HM, it is possible for some patients to have symptoms of both anterograde amnesia and retrograde amnesia (Damasio et al., 1985).

Task — Write down short case studies of two fictional patients. Describe their symptoms in a way that illustrates the difference between anterograde amnesia and retrograde amnesia.

As it happens, HM's main difficulties were forming new long-term memories (memories that last roughly more than 30 seconds). What made him interesting to cognitive neuropsychologists was that his symptoms were particularly severe and particularly pronounced when compared to other patients with anterograde amnesia symptoms.

Since these first reports HM has worked with over 100 researchers (Corkin, 2002) as they have attempted to understand and explain his symptoms. Importantly, this has influenced our theories of how memory might work.

Approaches to memory

In Chapter 3 you learned about an approach to memory proposed around the same time. To recap, Atkinson and Shiffrin (1968) developed a model of memory that argued for a sequence of three different types of memory, also called mental stores. From what you have learned in this chapter, you might like to think of these as modules. Most attention has been paid to the three separate stores that Atkinson and Shiffrin (1968) proposed: a sensory register; a short-term store; and a long-term store.

For our purposes here, we will focus on the short-term store and the long-term store. Atkinson and Shiffrin (1968) estimated that information is lost from the short-term store in about 30 seconds, unless it is rehearsed. It was argued that if the information was needed on an even more permanent basis, then it was 'copied' into the long-term store. This suggests that everything goes in one direction (from sensory register to short-term store to long-term store). Atkinson and Shiffrin (1968) also suggested that information could be copied from the long-term store into the short-term store if it was needed. This flow of information through the system is illustrated again in Figure 8.1.

Figure 8.1: *Flow of information through memory as described by Atkinson and Shiffrin (1968)*

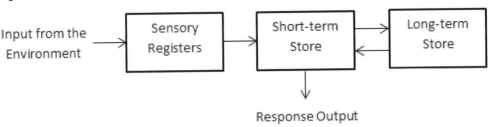

It is worth noting that HM also has relatively spared language abilities (e.g. Kensinger et al., 2001) despite his memory impairments. He is nevertheless impaired in the learning of new words (Gabrieli et al., 1988).

So what does patient HM teach us about this model? Well, testing indicated that HM's short-term memory is relatively spared (e.g. Prisko, 1963; Sidman et al., 1968; Wickelgren, 1968). The issue is that information was rarely transferred from short-term memory into long-term memory. It could therefore be argued that it is this part of the system that is damaged. However, an important point here is that learning was rare but not absent completely.

Milner (1962) also reported that HM was able to learn some new motor skills, despite having no memory for the testing sessions and generally severe memory impairments. This relatively preserved ability was confirmed in later studies (e.g. Corkin, 1968; Savoy and Gabrieli, 1991) and is crucial for the impact that HM has had on our understanding. In order to account for this finding we need to consider how we understand the structure of long-term memory.

In the model proposed by Atkinson and Shiffrin (1968), the long-term store is a single component in the overall system. If this was the case, then HM's relatively preserved learning of motor skills, in the absence of awareness, would not be predicted. The suggestion is, therefore, that the long-term store may need to be divided into multiple memory systems. The case of HM provides some support for distinguishing between at least two types of long-term memory: procedural memory and declarative memory.

Task ― In your own words, explain why the model of memory proposed by Atkinson and Shiffrin (1968) is not suitable for explaining HM's symptoms.

Procedural memory vs. declarative memory

The distinction between procedural memory and declarative memory, in the case of memory impairments, is an important one (e.g. Cohen and Squire, 1980). It has been suggested that procedural memory is a system that is used to remember 'how' – for example, how you drive a car and how you hold a pen. Importantly, it is a memory that can be seen through actions that are performed differently based upon experience. In contrast, declarative memory is characterised by 'knowing that'. This is evidenced through explicit conscious knowledge that can be expressed. A pub quiz and an exam are examples of declarative memory tests.

Let's consider this now in terms of the example of HM. Remember that HM had extreme difficulty in remembering any facts or events after his operation (anterograde amnesia). However, HM was also able to learn some new motor skills although he couldn't remember doing so (e.g. Milner, 1962). In terms of procedural memory and declarative memory, it can be argued that HM has damage to his declarative memory (knowing that he had learned it) but not to his procedural memory, hence his ability to acquire new motor skills. This pattern of sparing and impairments is further observed with many different amnesic patients (see Squire, 1992; Gabrieli, 1998 for reviews), although none to the same extent as HM. The distinction between procedural memory and declarative memory therefore provides a better account of the cognitive neuropsychological data than the idea of a single long-term memory store.

Critical thinking activity

Knowing how but not knowing that

Critical thinking focus: critical and creative thinking

Key question: *How can we test whether DW has spared procedural memory?*

In this chapter you have learned that cognitive neuropsychologists use tests to help them understand the causes of impairments. As a division of cognitive psychology, the focus is on working out the cognitive processes that may be affected. While testing may begin with standard tests, as more is learned about specific symptoms researchers are forced to create new and novel tests to further explore the causes of a patient's impairments. This critical thinking activity involves you designing your own task to assess the following fictional patient.

DW is a 35-year-old man who has suffered a trauma to the head following a motor-cycle accident. DW has difficulty forming new memories although he can remember events from 12 months before the accident. Initial tests indicate that he has all the characteristics you might expect of anterograde amnesia. Research suggests that despite being unable to remember new events since the accident, he may be able to learn new information that he cannot express explicitly. You and your research team want to explore this further but don't have access to any standard tests that look at this specifically. You must therefore design your own task to use with DW.

On a piece of paper, design a task that you could give to DW to test his ability to learn new information. Design a task that does not require him to say out loud what he has learned. The last part is important because we want to test for procedural memory (knowing how) rather than declarative memory (knowing that). When you design your task you will need to consider several different aspects.

Measures. Think about what it is specifically you would measure (this may be how long he takes to do it, how many he gets correct or the types of errors he makes).

Materials. Specify any materials you might need. (Would you use pen and paper, images on a computer screen, or something else?)

Procedure. Write down what will happen in a step-by-step fashion. Think about what he will be told, and how long he will be given for each part of the task. You might find it useful to draw a diagram to illustrate your intentions.

Once you have designed your new task, the last thing to do is write down what you would expect to find. This is important because it will help you decide if your task would actually look at what you are interested in. Write down what you would expect to happen if he had a spared procedural memory. Then write down what you would expect to happen if he had an impaired procedural memory. For your test to work, this second prediction has to be different from the first. In writing these predictions, you might also want to consider whether you would need to test some people without his impairments to compare DW with (a control group).

Critical thinking review

This activity helps develop your critical and creative thinking skills. Creating new and novel methods of testing predictions is harder than it sounds, yet it is an important part of an intensive investigation. The task you just completed was based on a real problem faced by researchers interested in HM, and other anterograde amnesics.

The solution used by Corkin (1968) was to train HM on tracing a picture of a star while looking at the paper in a mirror. You might want to try this yourself; it is not as easy as it sounds but it can be learned through practice. Other researchers have also tested whether amnesics can learn more than just motor skills such as artificial grammar (e.g. Knowlton et al., 1992). There have been more solutions than these two examples. Importantly, in these tests the learning was demonstrated by improved performance after experience despite no explicit knowledge of what had been learned. It is in this way that the learning is procedural rather than declarative.

It does not matter if your solution was the same as either of these, as there is rarely just one solution for this sort of problem. By simply trying you will have started to develop your critical and creative skills. These skills are important skills to develop. The human mind is incredibly complex and we know relatively little about it. Cognitive psychology, like most psychology, involves a lot of exploration for which we often have to design our own tools. Creative thinking about these tools enables us to make important, and sometimes unexpected, discoveries.

Other skills you may have used in this activity include: analysing and evaluating; and reflection.

In this section of the chapter we have looked in detail at one patient, HM, and asked what we can learn about the normal mind from his symptoms. The example of HM, and other anterograde amnesics, is very important because it changed the way we thought about long-term memory. The wealth of evidence from unimpaired individuals and animal studies further support these ideas (see Squire, 1992). However, the example provided in this instance is only of the impact single dissociations may have on an area. As a further example, we will now consider visual information processing and the impact of a double dissociation. Specifically, we will focus on how we understand the organisation of visual processing.

Visual form agnosia

In this section of the chapter we will learn how a double dissociation has helped develop a theoretical approach in the field of visual perception. If you have read Chapter 5 of this book, then you will be familiar with some of the questions that have been addressed about perception by cognitive psychologists. For example, psychologists have asked how we perceive objects, interpret visual patterns and are fooled by visual illusions. Another important development in the last 20 years has been an increased interest in the relationship between perception and action. A small number of case studies have made an important contribution to this development and you will learn about these shortly. However, first you must briefly learn about one approach to understanding how our mind uses information from visual processing.

Visual information processing

We will begin by taking a short detour into how the brain is organised (**physiology**). The physiology of the visual system can be roughly considered as separate pathways. These pathways are also referred to as 'streams'. They are known to be highly connected to each other but there are two main streams: the dorsal stream and the ventral stream. While the position of the streams is not important for our discussion, it may be worth noting that the terms 'dorsal' and 'ventral' refer to their relative positions in the brain.

It was Schneider (1967, 1969) who noted that as well as the streams being physiologically different, they may play very different roles in cognition. More specifically, it was suggested that one of the streams might help answer the question *What is it?* while the other might help answer the question *Where is it?* Later work by Ungerleider and Mishkin (1982) further supported this distinction, proposing that the dorsal stream is responsible for the 'where' question and the ventral stream is responsible for the 'what' question. Milner et al. (1991) proposed an alternative interpretation that was heavily influenced by patients with carbon monoxide poisoning. The symptoms of one patient in particular, DF, had an important impact upon this.

DF

Originally reported by Milner et al. (1991), DF had acquired problems processing visual information after suffering from carbon monoxide poisoning in her flat in Italy. Having emerged from her coma, she underwent rigorous testing both at the University of Turin at Novara, in Italy, and the

University of St Andrews, in Scotland. One of the reasons that DF was so interesting was that her problems affected many of her perceptual abilities. This included impairments to motion perception; depth perception; shape perception; figure/ground segregation; and perception of brightness. More generally, this has been labelled visual form agnosia (e.g. Benson and Greenberg, 1969), and the deficits of DF were severe. Having studied her symptoms, Milner et al. (1991) suggested that DF's difficulties could be understood in terms of damage to the ventral stream (the 'what' pathway).

Importantly, Milner et al. (1991) reported that DF was unimpaired in performing some actions, even though these actions relied upon the information she could not report. For example, DF was unable to report the orientation of a slot. Yet, when DF reached for the slot, the way she moved her hand matched the slot accurately. Similarly, although she was unable to accurately perceive solid rectangular objects, DF reached and grasped them as if she could (Goodale et al., 1991). This information is fascinating because it would suggest a dissociation between using visual information to perceive the world and using visual information to act upon the world. Indeed, this was how Milner and Goodale (1995) proposed the dorsal and ventral streams should be understood: the ventral stream processing 'what' information, and the dorsal stream proposing 'how' rather than 'where'. This idea of 'what' can also be called perception-related visual processing, and this idea of 'how' can also be called action-related visual processing.

Task ┐ In a short list, summarise the main differences between the dorsal stream and the ventral stream of visual information processing.

This pattern of impaired perception-related visual processing with spared action-related visual processing has been studied with DF in great depth (e.g. Goodale et al., 1994). It has also been complemented by another patient, JS, who shares a similar pattern of spared and impaired abilities following a stroke (Karnath et al., 2009), as well as SB who has similar symptoms after a lesion (Dijkerman et al., 2004). However, this only demonstrates a single dissociation.

Optic ataxia

You have learned already that a single dissociation can only teach us so much. The suggestion from the case of DF is that there are separate streams for perception-related visual processing and action-related visual processing (e.g. Milner and Goodale, 1995). An important aspect of this argument is that there is a double dissociation with another set of symptoms. To establish this double dissociation we must look at patients with the symptoms of optic ataxia.

Optic ataxia is associated with the dorsal stream and is characterised by difficulties when reaching and grasping objects but being able to correctly recognise them (e.g. Garcin et al., 1967; Vighetto,

1980). As we can see, this is the opposite pattern to that recorded about DF: able to act upon visual information, but difficulties in recognising objects. Given the logic of double dissociations that you have learned about, it should be clear that this supports the argument that 'what' and 'how' information are processed relatively separately.

Interestingly, Milner et al. (1999) have also reported that this impaired reaching and grasping ability with optic ataxia is improved after a delay. It is argued that this occurs because the patients are using information from their memories to execute their actions and that this ability to use memory to guide visual action is spared. This position is further supported by data from DF, whose actions were impaired when a short delay was introduced (Milner and Goodale, 1995), and has been found more broadly with patients with optic ataxia. Patients with optic ataxia don't avoid obstacles in experiments when they reach to pick something up (Schindler et al., 2004) while patients with visual form agnosia do (Rice et al., 2006). The implications of this are that the ventral stream ('what') makes use of long-term memories, also referred to as stored knowledge. Hence, patients with spared ventral streams (optic ataxia) can perform tasks after a delay. The other implication is that the dorsal stream ('how') is more immediate and mainly makes use of short-term memories.

This double dissociation between the severe form of visual agnosia, as most clearly demonstrated by DF (e.g. Milner et al., 1991), and optic ataxia (e.g. Perenin and Vighetto, 1983) is therefore important for at least two reasons. First, it supports the view that the dorsal and ventral streams may be used for action-related visual processing and perception-related visual processing respectively. This builds upon the initial 'what' and 'where' distinctions (e.g. Schneider, 1967, 1969; Ungerleider and Mishkin, 1982). Second, it suggests that the ventral stream is 'knowledge-based', making use of long-term memories (e.g. Milner and Goodale, 1995) while the dorsal stream makes use of more temporary representations (e.g. Milner et al. 1999). This would explain why patients with optic ataxia are better at reaching for objects after a delay, and why the reverse is true with DF.

The case of DF and optic ataxia is therefore a useful demonstration of how a cognitive neuropsychological double dissociation can influence the development of how we understand visual information processing.

Skill builder activity

Actions without perception and perceptions without actions

Transferable skill focus: teamwork

Key question: *How clear cut is the double dissociation between optic ataxia and visual form agnosia?*

In this chapter you have learned about a double dissociation between some of the symptoms of optic ataxia and some of the symptoms of visual form agnosia. It has been suggested that patterns of sparing and impairments associated with these syndromes might indicate that we have distinct action-related visual processing and perception-related visual processing. You have learned already that focusing on just syndromes can sometimes oversimplify the issue. In this skill builder you will use the research skills you have developed throughout this book to investigate how clear cut this distinction is. Importantly, you will also develop your teamwork skills.

As this activity is designed to develop your teamwork skills, you will need to work with at least one other person. This means that you will have to negotiate between you who will take responsibility for the different parts of the task, who will negotiate deadlines and how you will share information, as well as communicating effectively what you have found to the other person.

With this activity we will make use of the internet to explore research findings about both visual form agnosia and optic ataxia. If you are working in a pair, then I suggest that one of you focuses upon visual form agnosia, while the other focuses on optic ataxia. If there are more than two of you, then decide between you what each of you will focus upon.

On a computer, open up an internet browser (such as Internet Explorer, Firefox or Google Chrome) and navigate to a suitable search tool (such as www.google.co.uk or www.bing.co.uk). You will then need to find a database of research abstracts to use. A research abstract is a short summary of a piece of research that tells you what the problem was that was being researched, what the researchers did, what they found, and what they think it means. It is possible to find databases of research abstracts that are just from psychological research. One well-known database is PsycINFO® but you may need to pay to use it. If you are currently studying at university or college, then where you are studying may already be paying for you to have access and it is worth checking with them to see if you can use it. There are currently freely available databases such as PubMED that are not specific to just psychological research but are more helpful than a general search of the whole internet. If you do not have access to PsycINFO®, then use a search tool to find the website for PubMED.

Now that you are on a website that provides a database of research abstracts, use the search facility to look for your topic area. Remember that at least one person is investigating 'visual form agnosia' and at least one other person is investigating 'optic ataxia'. A long list of titles of research will be displayed. You may, or may not, have to click on the title to be able to read the whole abstract; this depends upon the database that you are using. Choose four or five of these abstracts to read in more detail, perhaps using the titles to guide your choice. When you read the abstracts you will need to note down two things in particular.

Behaviours, skills or abilities that are spared.

Behaviours, skills or abilities that are impaired.

Make sure you repeat this exercise for at least four or five abstracts (or as many as you like). Now you will need to compare your findings with the other people you are working with. You may find it useful to write all of the findings on a piece of paper or a word processing document. From the evidence you have found, discuss whether there is a clear difference between the patterns of sparing and impairment between optic ataxia and visual form agnosia. Have you managed to find any areas of overlap or similarity as well?

Skill builder review

This activity helps develop your teamwork skills through researching. Importantly, it is not possible to complete this task unless everyone in the team does their bit. You also gained experience of sharing information that you have found, and discussing these findings with a specific objective in mind. These are all important skills to develop because, in the world of work, we often complete tasks in teams, with every member of the team playing a vital role. Being able to work within a team, communicating effectively and negotiating tasks appropriately, are therefore invaluable skills to have.

Other skills you may have used in this activity include: information technology; organisational skills; decision making, and analysing and evaluating.

Assignments

1. Describe the defining characteristics and principles of cognitive neuropsychology. Clearly explain the relevant methods and assumptions in this area, and illustrate your points with examples.

2. Evaluate what we can learn about memory when considering patient HM. Describe, with examples, his symptoms, and explain how this informs theories of memory. Discuss the strengths of this approach as well as identifying any limitations or weaknesses.

3. Compare and contrast the symptoms of DF and those of patients with optic ataxia. Provide examples and explain how this has developed our understanding of visual information processing. Highlight any limitations and areas for further research.

Summary: what you have learned

You have learned that cognitive neuropsychology is a division of cognitive psychology that is concerned with understanding a patient's symptoms in terms of damage to cognitive processes. This information can also be used to develop theories about unimpaired cognitive processes. To do this we must assume that the mind is organised in the same way for everyone (universality), that it is divided into independent modules (modularity), that damaging a module doesn't change the overall system (transparency), and that modules can be taken away but not added (subtractivity). As an area of research it makes relatively high use of single-case studies and of double dissociations.

You now know about patient HM who has severe memory impairments for new facts and events (anterograde amnesia). You have learned that, despite the severe impairments, HM is able to learn some new information if learning does not require an explicit response. This has provided support for distinguishing between multiple types of long-term memory, and between procedural memory and declarative memory in particular.

You have also learned that theories of visual perception have been developed on the basis of cognitive neuropsychological evidence. Specifically, you have learned about an important distinction between a ventral stream of information processing and a dorsal stream of information processing, which are characterised by perception-related visual processing and action-related visual processing. You have found out about some symptoms of patient DF and some symptoms of optic ataxia that have allowed us to establish a double dissociation. This double dissociation supports the idea of the relatively distinct roles of the streams.

When completing the critical thinking activity, you will have learned a little about what it is like to design new tasks for assessment purposes. This has begun to develop your critical and creative thinking abilities. You have also had the opportunity to develop your teamwork skills through collaboratively researching in the skill builder activity.

Further reading

Ellis, AW and Young, AW (1996) *Human cognitive neuropsychology: a textbook with readings*. 2nd edition. Hove: Psychology Press.

The seminal textbook in this area, it still provides an excellent introduction through carefully chosen readings from classic studies.

Kolb, B and Whishaw, IQ (2008) *Fundamentals of human neuropsychology*. 6th edition. New York: Worth Publishers.

A comprehensive and reliable text that provides a broader coverage of the field, presented in a readable way.

McCarthy, RA and Warrington, EK (2012) *Cognitive neuropsychology: a clinical introduction.* 2nd edition. London: Academic Press.

An updated alternative to Kolb and Whishaw (2008), this provides an accessible introduction to the broad subject area from a clinical perspective.

Glossary

abstract	(1) different from concrete reality; (2) a summary of a scientific article/text.
activation	mental energy that is assigned to a given mental representation.
analogy	comparison between two things based on their similarities.
behaviourism	a school of psychology based solely on observable and quantifiable behaviours.
bottom-up processing	processing that is based on information provided by the environment.
boundary conditions	the circumstances in which a phenomenon can no longer be found, or a theory no longer applies.
circular reasoning	reasoning in which support for a statement falsely comes from restating it in different terms.
cognition	information processing in the mind.
cognitive neuropsychology	a subdivision of cognitive psychology that uses data from individuals with damage or injury to the brain.
cognitive psychology	the scientific study of the mind as an information processor.
cognitive revolution	a period of time in which cognitive psychology developed rapidly as an area of study.
concrete	existing physically (compare with *abstract*).
confirmation bias	a tendency to more readily accept ideas that are personally agreed with.
connectionist	a way of modelling the mind in terms of interconnected units.
conscious	occurring with awareness.
context	the set of circumstances that surround a behaviour or phenomenon.
context-dependent	a behaviour or phenomenon that is only observable in a given context.
demand characteristics	when participants' behaviour is changed because of their interpretation of the purpose of the research.
dependent variable	the variable, or variables, that have been measured by the researcher.
domain	a subdivision of a concept (e.g. sensory domain).

domain-specific	information processing that is limited to a given domain(s).
ecological validity	extent to which something is similar to 'real life' situations.
ecologically valid	see *ecological validity*.
empirical	able to be demonstrated through experience of experiment.
episodic memory	explicit memory for autobiographical events.
explicit memory	memory that can be consciously articulated.
extrinsic context	context that is provided by external circumstances (compare to *intrinsic context*).
falsifiability	the possibility that a hypothesis or theory can be shown to be false.
generalisability	extent to which something can be generalised to other contexts.
generalise	the property of applying to other contexts.
Gestalt	indicates a particular approach to psychology that argues for the study of 'wholes' rather than individual parts.
Gestalt psychology	a branch of psychology associated with the *Gestalt* movement, originating in Berlin.
heuristic(s)	a general rule or principle that guides behaviour.
hypotheses	explanations of phenomena under specified conditions.
implicit memory	memory that alters behaviour without conscious awareness.
independent variable	the variable, or variables, that have been intentionally manipulated by the researcher.
intrinsic context	context that originates internally (e.g. mood).
mental lexicon	a mental store of representations of words.
mind	both conscious and unconscious information processing that influence behaviour.
modalities	belonging to a particular group (e.g. sensory modalities).
modular	consisting of modules.
module	a self-contained unit that supports a specific task.
morphemes	the smallest unit in a word with meaning.

neurobiological	of the nervous system (including the brain).
neurobiologists	those who study the biology of the nervous system.
neuroscientists	those who study the nervous system.
objective	not influenced by personal interpretation.
objective measure	a measure that is not influenced by personal interpretation (compare to *subjective measure*).
objectivity	see *objective*.
operational definition	a precise definition of how a concept is measured.
orthography	written structure (e.g. of a word).
paradigm	an example that acts as a model.
parallel model	an information-processing model based on some, or all, of the stages occurring in parallel.
phenomena	plural of phenomenon, meaning observable events.
phonology	the sounds associated with language.
physiology	the functions of a living organism or any of its parts.
predictive power	the extent to which a theory can be used to create testable hypotheses.
pseudoscience	claims presented as scientific but without scientific foundation.
reaction time	a measurement of how long it takes to initiate or complete a behaviour.
replicability	that research findings can be replicated.
scientific method	investigation of phenomena through careful observation and experimentation related to hypotheses or theories.
semantic memory	explicit memory for facts and general knowledge about the world.
semantics	the study of meanings (e.g. of words).
serial model	an information-processing model based on a series of consecutive stages.
subjective measure	a measure that is influenced by personal interpretation (compare to *objective measure*).
syntactics	the study of the order or system of things.

theories	proposed explanations for behaviours or phenomena, usually consisting of several propositions or hypotheses.
thought experiment	a mental test of a hypothesis.
threshold	the point at which there is sufficient mental energy to initiate an effect.
top-down processing	processing that is based on information provided internally.
unconscious	occurring without awareness.
variable	aspect that can be varied or changed (see also independent variable, and dependent variable).

References

Ahlum-Heath, ME and DiVesta, FJ (1986) The effect of conscious controlled verbalization cognitive strategy on transfer in problem solving. *Memory and Cognition,* 14: 281–85.

Albert, ML and Bear, D (1974) Time to understand: a case study of word deafness with reference to the role of time in auditory comprehension. *Journal of Neurology,* 97: 373–84.

Allport, DA (1980) Attention and performance, in Claxton, G (ed.) *Cognitive psychology: new directions* (112–53). London: Routledge & Kegan Paul.

Allport, DA, Antonis, B and Reynolds, P (1972) On the division of attention: a disproof of the single channel hypothesis. *Quarterly Journal of Experimental Psychology,* 24: 225–35.

Alm, H and Nilsson, L (1994) Changes in driver behaviour as a function of handsfree mobile phones: a simulator study. *Accident, Analysis & Prevention,* 26: 441–51.

Amado, S and Ulupinar, P (2005) The effects of conversation on attention and peripheral detection: is talking with a passenger and talking on the cell phone different? *Transportation Research Part F, Traffic Psychology and Behaviour,* 8: 383–95.

Anderson, JR (1983) *The architecture of cognition.* Cambridge, MA: Harvard University Press.

Anderson, JR, Bothell, D, Byrne, MD, Douglass, S, Lebiere, C, and Qin, Y (2004) An integrated theory of the mind. *Psychological Review,* 111: 1036–60.

Andrews, S (1989) Frequency and neighborhood effects on lexical access: activation or search? *Journal of Experimental Psychology: Learning, Memory, and Cognition,* 15: 802–14.

Andrews, S (1992) Frequency and neighborhood effects on lexical access: lexical similarity or orthographic redundancy? *Journal of Experimental Psychology: Learning, Memory, and Cognition,* 18: 234–54.

Arnon, I and Snider, N (2010) More than words: frequency effects for multi-word phrases. *Journal of Memory and Language,* 62: 67–82.

Atkinson, RC and Shiffrin, RM (1968) Human memory: a proposed system and its control processes, in Spence, KW (ed.) *The psychology of learning and motivation: advances in research and theory, volume 2* (89–195). New York: Academic Press.

Awh, E and Pashler, H (2000) Evidence for split attentional foci. *Journal of Experimental Psychology: Human Perception and Performance,* 26: 834–46.

Baddeley, AD (1982) Implications of neuropsychological evidence for theories of normal memory. *Philosophical Transactions of the Royal Society B: Biological Sciences,* 298: 59–72.

Baddeley, AD and Hitch, GJ (1974) Working memory, in Bower, GQ (ed.) *Recent advances in learning and memory: volume 8* (47–89). New York: Academic Press.

Baddeley, AD and Hitch, GJ (1977) Recency re-examined, in S Dornic (ed.) *Attention and performance: volume VI* (647–67). Hillsdale NJ: Lawrence Erlbaum Associates.

Bahrick, HP and Phelps, E (1987) Retention of Spanish vocabulary over eight years. *Journal of Experimental Psychology: Learning, Memory, and Cognition,* 13: 344–49.

Baker, JR, Bezance, JB, Zellaby, E and Aggleton, JP (2004) Chewing gum can produce context-dependent effects upon memory. *Appetite,* 43: 207–10.

Barsalou, LW (1982) Context-independent and context-dependent information in concepts. *Memory and Cognition,* 10: 82–93.

Barsalou, LW (1987) The instability of graded structure: implications for the nature of concepts, in Neisser, U (ed.) *Concepts and conceptual development: ecological and intellectual factors in categorization* (101–40). Cambridge: Cambridge University Press.

Barsalou, LW (1989) Intraconcept similarity and its implications for interconcept similarity, in Vosniadou, S and Ortony, A (eds) *Similarity and analogical reasoning* (76–121). New York: Cambridge University Press.

Beck, IL and Carpenter, PA (1986) Cognitive approaches to understanding reading: implications for instructional practice. *American Psychologist,* 41: 1098–105.

Behrens, R (2002) *False colors: art, design and modern camouflage.* Dysart, Iowa: Bobolink Books.

Benson, DF and Greenberg, JP (1969) Visual form agnosia: a specific deficit in visual discrimination. *Archives of Neurology,* 20: 82–89.

Bever, TG (1970) The cognitive basis for linguistic structures, in Hayes, R (ed.) *Cognition and language development* (279–362). New York: Wiley and Sons.

Bernstein, IH and Eriksen, CW (1965) Effects of 'subliminal' prompting on paired-associate learning. *Journal of Experimental Research in Personality,* 1: 33–38.

Biederman, I (1987) Recognition-by-components: a theory of human image understanding. *Psychological Review,* 94: 115–47.

Block, N (1995) On a confusion about a function of consciousness. *The Behavioral and Brain Sciences* 18: 227–72.

Bowden, EM (1985) Information access in problem solving: constraints on search in the problem space. *Memory and Cognition,* 13: 280–86.

Bransford, JD and Stein, BS (1993) The IDEAL problem solver. 2nd edition. New York: Freeman.

Broadbent, DE (1958) *Perception and communication.* New York: Oxford University Press.

Broadbent, DE (1982) Task combination and selective intake of information. *Acta Psychologica,* 50: 253–90.

Brown, GDA and Lewandowsky, S (2010) Forgetting in memory models: arguments against trace decay and consolidation failure, in Della Salla, S (ed.) *Forgetting* (49–75). New York: Psychology Press.

Brown, GDA, Neath, I and Chater, N (2007) A temporal ratio model of memory. *Psychological Review,* 114: 539–76.

Bruner, JS (1957) On perceptual readiness. *Psychological Review,* 64: 123–52.

Bülthoff, HH and Edelman, S (1992) Psychophysical support for a 2-D view interpolation theory of object recognition. *Proceedings of the National Academy of Science,* 89: 60–64.

Caramazza, A (1984) The logic of neuropsychological research and the problem of patient classification in aphasia. *Brain & Language,* 21: 9–20.

Caramazza, A (1986) On drawing inferences about the structure of normal cognitive systems from the analysis of patterns of impaired performance: the case for single-patient studies. *Brain and Cognition,* 5: 41–66.

Caramazza, A and McCloskey, M (1988) The case for single-patient studies. *Cognitive Neuropsychology,* 5: 517–27.

Carroll, JB and White, MN (1973) Age-of-acquisition norms for 220 picturable nouns. *Journal of Verbal Learning and Verbal Behavior,* 12: 563–76.

Cattell, JM (1895) Measurement of the accuracy of recollection. *Science,* 20: 761–76.

Campion, J, Latto, R and Smith, YM (1983) Is blindsight an effect of scattered light, spared cortex, and near-threshold vision? *Behavioral and Brain Sciences,* 6: 423–86.

Chalmers, DJ (1996) *The conscious mind: in search of a fundamental theory.* New York: Oxford University Press.

Chase, WG and Simon, HA (1973) Perception in chess. *Cognitive Psychology,* 4: 55–81.

Cheesman, J and Merikle, PM (1986) Distinguishing conscious from unconscious perceptual processes. *Canadian Journal of Psychology*, 40: 343–67.

Chen, Z (2002) Analogical problem solving: a hierarchical analysis of procedural similarity. *Journal of Experimental Psychology: Learning, Memory, and Cognition*, 28: 81–98.

Cherry, EC (1953) Some experiments on the recognition of speech, with one and with two ears. *The Journal of the Acoustical Society of America*, 25: 975–79.

Clancy, SA, McNally, RJ, Schacter, DL, Lenzenweger, MF and Pitman, RK (2002) Memory distortion in people reporting abduction by aliens. *Journal of Abnormal Psychology*, 111: 455–61.

Clifford, CWG, Arabzadeh, E and Harris, JA (2008) Getting technical about awareness. *Trends in Cognitive Sciences*, 12: 54–58.

Cohen, NJ and Squire, L (1980) Preserved learning and retention of pattern-analyzing skill in amnesia: dissociation of knowing how and knowing that. *Science*, 210: 207–10.

Collett, C, Clarion, A, Morel, M, Chapon, A and Petit, C (2009) Physiological and behavioural changes associated to the management of secondary tasks while driving. *Applied Ergonomics*, 40: 1041–46.

Collett, C, Guillot, A and Petit, C (2010) Phoning while driving I: a review of epidemiological, psychological, behavioural and physiological studies. *Ergonomics*, 53: 589–601.

Coltheart, M (2001) Assumptions and methods in cognitive neuropsychology, in B Rapp (ed.) *Handbook of cognitive neuropsychology*. New York: Psychology Press.

Coltheart, M, Davelaar, E, Jonasson, JT and Besner, D (1977). Access to the internal lexicon, in Dornic, S (ed.) *Attention and Performance VI* (535–55). Hillsdale, NJ: Erlbaum.

Corkin, S (1968) Acquisition of motor skill after bilateral medial temporal-lobe excision. *Neuropsychologia*, 6: 225–64.

Corkin, S (2002) What's new with the amnesic patient H.M.? *Nature Reviews Neuroscience*, 3: 153–60.

Craik, FIM and Lockhart, RS (1972) Levels of processing: a framework for memory research. *Journal of Verbal Learning and Verbal Behavior*, 11: 671–84.

Craik, FIM and Lockhart, RS (1990) Levels of processing: a retrospective commentary on a framework for memory research. *Canadian Journal of Psychology*, 44: 87–112.

Croft, W and Cruse, DA (2004) *Cognitive linguistics*. Cambridge: Cambridge University Press.

Crundall, D, Bains, M, Chapman, P and Underwood, G (2005) Regulating conversation during driving: a problem for mobile telephones? *Transportation Research Part F: Traffic Psychology and Behaviour*, 8: 197–211.

Dahl, H (1979) Word frequencies of spoken American English. Detroit, MI: Verbatim.

Damasio, AR, Eslinger, PJ, Damasio, H, Van Hoesen, GW and Cornell, S (1985) Multimodal amnesic syndrome following bilateral temporal and basal forebrain damage. *Archives of Neurology*, 42: 252–59.

Daneman, M and Carpenter, PA (1980) Individual differences in working memory and reading. *Journal of Verbal Learning and Verbal Behavior*, 19: 450–66.

de Gelder, B, Vroomen, J, Pourtois, G and Weiskrantz, L (1999) Non-conscious recognition of affect in the absence of striate cortex. *Neuroreport*, 18: 3759–63.

Deese, J (1959) Influence of inter-item associative strength upon immediate free recall. *Psychological Reports*, 5: 305–12.

Dell, GS (1986) A spreading-activation theory of retrieval in sentence production. *Psychological Review*, 93: 283–321.

Dell, GS and O'Seagdha, PG (1992) Stages of lexical access in language production. *Cognition*, 42: 287–314.

Destrebecqz, A and Cleeremans, A (2001) Can sequence learning be implicit? New evidence with the process dissociation procedure. *Psychonomic Bulletin & Review,* 8: 343–50.

Deutsch, JA and Deutsch, D (1963) Attention: some theoretical considerations. *Psychological Review,* 70: 80–90.

Dienes, Z and Scott, R (2005) Measuring unconscious knowledge: distinguishing structural knowledge and judgment knowledge. *Psychological Research,* 69: 338–51.

Dienes, Z and Seth, A (2010) Gambling on the unconscious: a comparison of wagering and confidence ratings as measures of awareness in an artificial grammar task. *Consciousness and Cognition,* 19: 674–81.

Dienes, Z, Altmann, G, Kwan, L and Goode, A (1995) Unconscious knowledge of artificial grammars is applied strategically. *Journal of Experimental Psychology: Learning, Memory, and Cognition,* 21: 1322–38.

Dijkerman, HC, Le, S, Demonet, JF and Milner, AD (2004). Visuomotor performance in a patient with visual agnosia due to an early lesion. *Cognitive Brain Research,* 20: 12–25.

Ebbinghaus, H (1885) *Über das Gedächtnis.* Leipzig: Dunker. English translation in: Ebbinghaus, H (1913) *Memory: A Contribution to Experimental Psychology.* (HA Ruger and CE Bussenius, trans.) New York: Teachers College, Columbia University.)

Ebbinghaus, H (1913) *Memory: a contribution to experimental psychology.* (HA Ruger and CE Bussenius, trans.) New York: Teachers College, Columbia University.

Eich, E, Macaulay, D, and Ryan, L (1994) Mood dependent memory for events of the personal past. *Journal of Experimental Psychology: General,* 123: 201–15.

Ellis, AW and Young, AW (1988) *Human cognitive neuropsychology.* Hove: Lawrence Erlbaum.

Eltiti, S, Wallace, D and Fox, E (2005) Selective target processing: perceptual load or distractor salience? *Attention, Perception, & Psychophysics,* 67: 876–85.

Eriksen, BA and Eriksen, CW (1974) Effects of noise letters upon the identification of a target letter in a nonsearch task. *Attention, Perception, & Psychophysics,* 16: 143–49.

Eriksen, CW and St James, JD (1986) Visual attention within and around the field of focal attention: a zoom lens model. *Attention, Perception, & Psychophysics,* 40: 225–40.

Fitousi, D and Wenger, MJ (2011) Processing capacity under perceptual and cognitive load: a closer look at load theory. *Journal of Experimental Psychology: Human Perception and Performance,* 37: 781–98.

Fleishman, EA and Parker, JF (1962) Factors in the retention and relearning of perceptual-motor skill. *Journal of Experimental Psychology,* 64: 215–26.

Fodor, JA (1983) *The modularity of mind.* Cambridge, MA: MIT Press.

Forster, KI (1976) Accessing the mental lexicon, in Wales, RJ and Walker, EW (eds) *New approaches to language mechanisms.* Amsterdam: North-Holland.

Frazier, L (1979) *On comprehending sentences: syntactic parsing strategies.* Bloomington, IN: Indiana University Linguistics Club.

Freyd, JJ and Gleaves, DH (1996) 'Remembering' words not presented in lists: relevance to the current recovered/false memory controversy. *Journal of Experimental Psychology: Learning, Memory, and Cognition,* 22: 811–13.

Fromkin, VA (1971) The non-anomalous nature of anomalous utterances. *Language,* 47: 27–52.

Gabrieli, JDE (1998) Cognitive neuroscience of human memory. *Annual Reviews of Psychology,* 47: 87–115.

Gabrieli, JDE, Cohen, NJ and Corkin, S (1988) The impaired learning of semantic knowledge following bilateral medial temporal-lobe resection. *Brain and Cognition,* 7: 157–77.

Garcia-Larrea, L, Perchet, C, Perrin, F and Amenedo, E (2001) Interference of cellular phone conversations with visuo-motor tasks: an ERP study. *Journal of Psychophysiology,* 15: 14–21.

Garcin, R, Rondot, P and Recondo, J de (1967) Ataxie optique localisée aux deux hémichamps visuels homonymes gauches (étude clinique avec présentation d'un film). *Revista de Neurologia,* 116: 707–14.

Garrett, MF (1975) The analysis of sentence production, in Bower, GH (ed.) *The psychology of learning and motivation: volume 9* (133–77). New York: Academic Press.

Garrett, MF (1984) The organization of processing structure for language production: application to aphasic speech, in Caplan, D (ed.) *Biological perspectives on language* (173–93). Cambridge, MA: MIT Press.

Geiselman, ER, Fisher, RP, MacKinnon, DP, and Holland, HL (1985) Eyewitness memory enhancement in the police interview: cognitive retrieval mnemonics versus hypnosis. *Journal of Applied Psychology,* 70: 401–12.

Gibson, JJ (1966) *The senses considered as perceptual systems.* Oxford: Houghton Mifflin.

Gibson, JJ (1979) *The ecological approach to perception.* Boston, MA: Houghton Mifflin.

Gick, ML and Holyoak, KJ (1980) Analogical problem solving. *Cognitive Psychology,* 12: 306–55.

Gigerenzer, G and Brighton, H (2009). Homo heuristicus: why biased minds make better inferences. *Topics in Cognitive Science,* 1: 107–43.

Gigerenzer, G and Goldstein, DG (1996). Reasoning the fast and frugal way: models of bounded rationality. *Psychological Review,* 103: 650–69.

Godden, DR and Baddeley, AD (1975) Context-dependent memory in two natural environments: on land and underwater. *British Journal of Psychology,* 66: 325–31.

Godden, DR and Baddeley, AD (1980) When does context influence recognition memory? *British Journal of Psychology,* 71: 99–104.

Goodale, MA, Milner, AD, Jakobson, LS and Carey, DP (1991) A neurological dissociation between perceiving objects and grasping them. *Nature,* 349: 154–56.

Goldstein, DG and Gigerenzer, G (2002) Models of ecological rationality: the recognition heuristic. *Psychological Review,* 109: 75–90.

Goodale, MA, Jakobson, LS and Keillor, JM (1994) Differences in the visual control of pantomimed and natural grasping movements. *Neuropsychologia,* 32: 1159–78.

Gray, JA and Wedderburn, AAI (1960) Grouping strategies with simultaneous stimuli. *The Quarterly Journal of Experimental Psychology,* 12: 180–84.

Gregory, RL (1968) Perceptual illusions and brain models. *Proceedings of the Royal Society B,* 171: 179–296.

Gregory, RL (1972) Cognitive contours. *Nature,* 23: 51–52.

Gregory, RL (1980) Perceptions as hypotheses. *Philosophical Transactions of the Royal Society of London B,* 290: 181–97.

Gugerty, L, Rakauskas, M and Brooks, J (2004) Effects of remote and in-person verbal interactions on verbalization rates and attention to dynamic spatial scenes. *Accident Analysis and Prevention,* 36: 1029–43.

Hampton, JA (1981) An investigation of the nature of abstract concepts. *Memory and Cognition,* 9: 149–56.

Howe, CQ and Purves, D (2005) The Müller-Lyer illusion explained by the statistics of image–source relationships. *Proceedings of the National Academy of Sciences of the United States of America,* 102: 1234–39.

Hsiao, S-W and Chou, J-R (2006) A Gestalt-like perceptual measure for home page design using a fuzzy entropy approach. *International Journal of Human-Computer Studies,* 64: 137–56.

Huyck, CR (2009) A psycholinguistic model of natural language parsing implemented in simulated neurons. *Cognitive Neurodynamics,* 3: 317–30.

James, W (1890) *The principles of psychology: vol 1.* New York: Holt.

Jans, B, Peter, JC and De Weerd, P (2010) Visual spatial attention to multiple locations at once: the jury is still out. *Psychological Review,* 117: 637–82.

Johnston, WA and Heinz, SP (1978) Flexibility and capacity demands of attention. *Journal of Experimental Psychology: General,* 107: 420–35.

Juola, P and Plunkett, K (2000) Why double dissociations don't mean much, in Cohen, G, Johnston, RA and Plunkett, K (eds) *Exploring cognition: damaged brains and neural networks: readings in cognitive neuropsychology and connectionist modelling* (319–27). Hove: Psychology Press.

Kahneman, D (1973) *Attention and effort.* Englewood Cliffs, NJ: Prentice Hall.

Kahneman, D and Tversky, A (1973) On the psychology of prediction. *Psychological Review,* 80: 237–51.

Kahneman, D and Tversky, A (1979) Prospect theory: an analysis of decision under risk. *Econometrica,* 47: 263–91.

Karnath, HO, Rüter, J, Mandler, A and Himmelbach, M (2009) The anatomy of object recognition: visual form agnosia caused by medial occipitotemporal stroke. *The Journal of Neuroscience,* 29: 5854–62.

Kelly, MH and Bock, JK (1988) Stress in time. *Journal of Experimental Psychology: Human Perception and Performance,* 14: 389–403.

Kensinger, EA, Ullman, MT, and Corkin, S (2001) Bilateral medial temporal lobe damage does not affect lexical or grammatical processing: evidence from amnesic patient H.M. *Hippocampus,* 11: 347–60.

King, SM, Azzopardi, P, Cowey, A, Oxbury, J and Oxbury, S (1996) The role of light scatter in the residual visual sensitivity of patients with complete cerebral hemispherectomy. *Visual Neuroscience,* 13: 1–13.

Kingdom, FAA, Yoonessi, A and Gheorghiu, E (2007) The Leaning Tower illusion: a new illusion of perspective. *Perception,* 36: 475–77.

Knowlton, BJ, Ramus, SJ and Squire, LR (1992) Intact artificial grammar learning in amnesia: dissociation of classification learning and explicit memory for specific instances. *Psychological Science,* 3: 172–79.

Köhler, W (1925) *The mentality of apes.* New York: Harcourt, Brace and World.

Kramer, AF and Hahn, S (1995) Splitting the beam: distribution of attention over noncontiguous regions of the visual field. *Psychological Science,* 6: 381–86.

Kruschke, JK (1992) ALCOVE: an exemplar-based connectionist model of category learning. *Psychological Review,* 99: 22–44.

Kucera, H and Francis, WN (1967) Computational analysis of present-day American English. Providence, RI: Brown University Press.

Lamble, D, Kauranen, T, Laakso, M and Summala, H (1999) Cognitive load and detection thresholds in car following situations: safety implications for using mobile (cellular) telephones while driving. *Accident Analysis and Prevention,* 31: 617–23.

Lavie, N (1995) Perceptual load as a necessary condition for selective attention. *Journal of Experimental Psychology: Human Perception and Performance,* 21: 451–68.

Lavie, N (2000) Selective attention and cognitive control: dissociating attentional functions through different types of load, in Monsell, S and Driver, J (eds) *Attention and performance XVIII* (175–94). Cambridge, MA: MIT Press.

Lavie, N and Tsal, Y (1994) Perceptual load as a major determinant of the locus of selection in visual attention. *Attention, Perception & Psychophysics,* 56: 183–97.

Lavie, N, Hirst, A, de Fockert, JW and Viding, E (2004) Load theory of selective attention and cognitive control. *Journal of Experimental Psychology: General,* 133: 339–54.

Leippe, MR, Eisenstadt, D and Rauch, SM (2009) Cueing confidence in eyewitness identifications: influence of biased lineup instructions and pre-identification memory feedback under varying lineup conditions. *Law and Human Behavior,* 33: 194–212.

Levelt, WJM (1989) *Speaking: from intention to articulation.* Cambridge, MA: MIT Press.

Levelt, WJM, Schreifers, H, Vorberg, D, Meyer, AS, Pechmann, T and Havinga, J (1991) The time course of lexical access in speech production: a study of picture naming. *Psychological Review,* 98: 615–18.

Levelt, WJ, Roelofs, A and Meyer, AS (1999) A theory of lexical access in speech production. *The Behavioral Brain Sciences,* 22: 1–38.

Loftus, EF (1996) *Eyewitness testimony.* Cambridge, MA: Harvard University Press.

Loftus, EF and Palmer, JC (1974) Reconstruction of automobile destruction: an example of the interaction between language and memory. *Journal of Verbal Learning and Verbal Behavior,* 13: 585–89.

Logan, GD and Crump, MJC (2009) The left hand doesn't know what the right hand is doing: the disruptive effects of attention to the hands in skilled typing. *Psychological Science,* 10: 1296–300.

Logothetis, NK, Pauls, J and Poggio, T (1995) Shape representation in the inferior temporal cortex of monkeys. *Current Biology,* 5: 552–63.

MacDonald, MC, Pearlmutter, NJ and Seidenberg, MS (1994) The lexical nature of syntactic ambiguity resolution. *Psychological Review,* 101: 676–703.

Malt, BC and Smith, EE (1982) The role of familiarity in determining typicality. *Memory and Cognition,* 10: 69–75.

Marcel, AJ (1998) Blindsight and shape perception: deficit of visual consciousness or of visual function? *Brain,* 121: 1565–88.

Marr, D and Nishihara, HK (1978) Representation and recognition of the spatial organization of three-dimensional shapes. *Proceedings of the Royal Society B,* 200: 269–94.

Marslen-Wilson, WD (1987) Functional parallelism in spoken word-recognition. *Cognition,* 25: 71–102.

Marslen-Wilson, WD (1990) Activation, competition, and frequency in lexical access, in Altmann, GTM (ed.) *Cognitive models of speech processing: psycholinguistics and computational perspectives* (148–72). Cambridge, MA: MIT Press.

Marslen-Wilson, W and Tyler, LK (1980) The temporal structure of spoken language understanding. *Cognition,* 8: 1–71.

Marslen-Wilson, WD and Welsh, A (1978) Processing interactions and lexical access during word recognition in continuous speech. *Cognitive Psychology,* 10: 29–63.

McCloskey, ME and Glucksberg, S (1978) Natural categories: well defined or fuzzy sets? *Memory and Cognition,* 6: 462–72.

McDonald, SA and Shillcock, RC (2003) Eye movements reveal the on-line computation of lexical probabilities during reading. *Psychological Science,* 14: 648–52.

McKenna, SP and Glendon, AI (1985) Occupational first aid training: decay in cardiopulmonary resuscitation (CPR) skills. *Journal of Occupational Psychology,* 58: 109–17.

McLeod, P (1977) A dual task response modality effect: support for multiprocessor models of attention. *Quarterly Journal of Experimental Psychology,* 29: 651–67.

McMains, SA and Sommers, DC (2004) Multiple spotlights of attentional selection in human visual cortex. *Neuron,* 42: 677–86.

Mervis, CB and Pani, JR (1980) Acquisition of basic object categories. *Cognitive Psychology,* 12: 496–522.

Meyersburg, CA, Bogdan, R, Gallo, DA and McNally, RJ (2009) False memory propensity in people reporting recovered memories of past lives. *Journal of Abnormal Psychology,* 118: 399–404.

Miles, C and Hardman, E (1998) State-dependent memory produced by aerobic exercise. *Ergonomics,* 41: 20–28.

Miles, C and Johnson, AJ (2007) Chewing gum and context-dependent memory effects: a re-examination. *Appetite,* 48: 154–58.

Miller, GA (1956) The magic number seven, plus or minus two: some limits on our capacity for information processing. *Psychological Review,* 63: 81–93.

Milner, B (1962) Les troubles de la memoire accompagnant des lesions hippocampiques bilaterales, in *Physiologie de l'hippocampe* (257–72). Paris: Centre National de la Recherche Scientifique. English translation: Memory disturbance after bilateral hippocampal lesions in Milner, P and Glickman, S (eds) *Cognitive processes and the brain* (97–111), Princeton, NJ: Van Nostrand, 1965.

Milner, B (1966) Amnesia following operation on the temporal lobes, in Whitty, CWM and Zangwill, OL (eds) *Amnesia.* London: Butterworths.

Milner, AD and Goodale, MA (1995) *The visual brain in action.* Oxford: Oxford University Press.

Milner, AD, Perrett, DI, Johnston, RS, Benson, PJ, Jordan, TR, Heeley, DW, Bettucci, D, Mortara, F, Mutani, R, Terazzi, E and Davidson, DLW (1991) Perception and action in 'visual form agnosia'. *Brain,* 114: 405–28.

Milner, AD, Paulignan, Y, Dijkerman, HC, Michel, F and Jeannerod, M (1999) A paradoxical improvement of misreaching in optic ataxia: new evidence for two separate neural systems for visual localization. *Proceedings of the Royal Society B,* 266: 2225–29.

Morton, J (1969) Interaction of information in word recognition. *Psychological Review,* 76: 165–78.

Morton, J (1970) A functional model for memory, in Norman, DA (ed.) *Models of human memory.* New York: Academic Press.

Müller, MM, Malinowski, P, Gruber, T and Hillyard, SA (2003) Sustained division of the attentional spotlight. *Nature,* 424: 309–12.

Müller-Lyer, FC (1889) Optische urteilstäuschungen. Archiv für Anatomie und Physiologie, Physiologische Abteilung 2: 263–70. Optical illusions (RH Day and H Knuth, trans.). *Perception,* 10: 131–36.

Nagel, T (1974) What is it like to be a bat? *Philosophical Review,* 83: 435.

Nairne, JS (1990) A feature model of immediate memory. *Memory and Cognition,* 18: 251–69.

Nash, RA and Wade, KA (2008) Innocent but proven guilty: eliciting internalized false confessions using doctored-video evidence. *Applied Cognitive Psychology,* 23: 624–37.

Navon, D and Gopher, D (1979) On the economy of the human-processing system. *Psychological Review,* 86: 214–55.

Neath, I and Surprenant, AM (2003) *Human memory.* Belmont, CA: Wadsworth/Thompson.

Neisser, U (1967) *Cognitive psychology.* New York: Meredith.

Newell, BR and Shanks, DR (2004) On the role of recognition in decision making. *Journal of Experimental Psychology: Learning, Memory, and Cognition,* 30: 923–35.

Newell, A and Simon, HA (1972) *Human problem solving.* Englewood Cliffs, NJ: Prentice-Hall.

Norman, DA (1968) Toward a theory of memory and attention. *Psychological Review,* 75: 522–36.

Norman, DA and Bobrow, DG (1975) On data-limited and resource-limited processes. *Cognitive Psychology,* 7: 44–64.

Norman, KA and Schacter, DL (1997) False recognition in younger and older adults: exploring the characteristics of illusory memories. *Memory and Cognition,* 25: 838–48.

Nosofsky, RM (1986) Attention, similarity and the identification-categorization relationship. *Journal of Experimental Psychology: General,* 115: 39–57.

Nosofsky, RM (1991) Relation between the rational model and the context model of categorization. *Psychological Science,* 2: 416–21.

O'Rourke, TB and Holcomb, PJ (2002) Electrophysiological evidence for the efficiency of spoken word processing. *Biological Psychology,* 60: 121–50.

Overgaard, M (2011) Visual experience and blindsight: a methodological review. *Experimental Brain Research,* 209: 473–79.

Overgaard, M, Fehl, K, Mouridsen, K, Bergholt, B and Cleeremans, A (2008) Seeing without seeing? Degraded conscious vision in a blindsight patient. *PLoS ONE,* 3: 1–4.

Palmer, SE (1975) The effects of contextual scenes on the identification of objects. *Memory and Cognition,* 3: 519–26.

Palmer, SE (1992) Common region: a new principle of perceptual grouping. *Cognitive Psychology,* 24: 436–47.

Patterson, KE and Marcel, AJ (1977) Aphasia, dyslexia and the phonological coding of written words. *The Quarterly Journal of Experimental Psychology,* 29: 307–18.

Patterson, K, Lambon-Ralph, MA, Jefferies, E, Woollams, A, Jones, R, Hodges, JR and Rogers, TT (2006) 'Presemantic' cognition in semantic dementia: six deficits in search of an explanation. *Journal of Cognitive Neuroscience,* 18: 169–83.

Perenin, M-T and Vighetto, A (1983) Optic ataxia: a specific disorder in visuomotor coordination, in Hein, A and Jeannerod, M (eds) *Spatially oriented behavior* (305–26). New York: Springer.

Persaud, N and McLeod, P (2008) Wagering demonstrates subconscious processing in a binary exclusion task. *Consciousness and Cognition,* 17: 565–75.

Persaud, N, McLeod, P and Cowey, A (2007) Post-decision wagering objectively measures awareness. *Nature Neuroscience,* 10: 257–61.

Peterson, LR and Peterson, MJ (1959) Short-term retention of individual verbal items. *Journal of Experimental Psychology,* 58: 193–98.

Plaut, DC, McClelland, JL, Seidenberg, MS and Patterson, K (1996) Understanding normal and impaired word reading: computational principles in quasi-regular domains. *Psychological Review,* 103: 56–115.

Ponzo, M (1913) Rapports entre quelques illusions visuelles de contraste angulaire et l'appreciation de grandeur des astres a l'horizon. *Archives Italiennes de Biologie,* 58: 327–29.

Pöppel, E, Held, R and Frost, D (1973) Residual visual function after brain wounds involving the central pathways in man. *Nature,* 203: 295–96.

Posner, MI (1978) *Chronometric explorations of mind.* Englewood Heights, NJ: Erlbaum.

Posner, MI (1980) Orienting of attention. *Quarterly Journal of Experimental Psychology,* 32: 3–25.

Posner, MI, Snyder, CR and Davidson, BJ (1980) Attention and the detection of signals. *Journal of Experimental Psychology: General,* 109: 160–74.

Prisko, L (1963) *Short-term memory in cerebral damage.* Unpublished doctoral thesis, McGill University.

Ramsøy, TZ and Overgaard, M (2004) Introspection and subliminal perception. *Phenomenology and the Cognitive Sciences,* 3: 1–23.

Ratner, JB and Gleason, NB (1993) An orientation to psycholinguistic research, in Gleason, NB and Ratner, JB (eds) *Psycholinguistics* (1–41). New York: Harcourt.

Rayner, K and Duffy, SA (1986) Lexical complexity and fixation times in reading: effects of word frequency, verb complexity, and lexical ambiguity. *Memory & Cognition,* 14: 191–201.

Rayner, K and Pollatsek, A (1989) *The psychology of reading.* Englewood Cliffs, NJ: Prentice Hall.

Reali, F and Christiansen, MH (2007) Processing of relative clauses is made easier by frequency of occurrence. *Journal of Memory and Language,* 57: 1–23.

Reber, AS (1967) Implicit learning of synthetic languages: the role of instructional set. *Journal of Experimental Psychology: Human Learning and Memory,* 2: 88–94.

Rice, NJ, McIntosh, RD, Schindler, I, Mon-Williams, M, Démonet, J-F, and Milner, AD (2006) Intact automatic avoidance of obstacles in patients with visual form agnosia. *Experimental Brain Research,* 174: 176–88.

Riddoch, G (1917) Dissociation of visual perceptions due to occipital injuries, with especial reference to appreciation of movement. *Brain,* 40: 15–57.

Rips, LJ, Shoben, EJ and Smith, EE (1973) Semantic distance and the verification of sematic relations. *Journal of Verbal Learning and Verbal Behavior,* 12: 1–20.

Rock, I and Palmer, S (1990) The legacy of gestalt psychology. *Scientific American,* 263: 84–90.

Roediger, HL and McDermott, KB (1995) Creating false memories: remembering words not presented in lists. *Journal of Experimental Psychology: Learning, Memory, and Cognition,* 21: 803–14.

Rosch, E and Mervis, CB (1975) Family resemblances: studies in the internal structure of categories. *Cognitive Psychology,* 7: 573–605.

Saffran, EM (1982) Neuropsychological approaches to the study of language. *British Journal of Psychology,* 73: 317–37.

Sagi, D and Julesz, B (1985) 'Where' and 'what' in vision. *Science,* 228: 1217–19.

Sandberg, K, Timmermans, B, Overgaard, M and Cleeremans, A (2010) Measuring consciousness: is one measure better than the other? *Consciousness and Cognition,* 19: 1069–78.

Savage, LJ (1954) *The foundations of statistics.* New York: John Wiley.

Savoy, RL and Gabrieli, JDE (1991) Normal McCollough effect in Alzheimer's disease and global amnesia. *Perception and Psychophysics,* 49: 448–55.

Schindler, I, Rice, N, McIntosh, RD, Rossetti, Y, Vighetto, A, and Milner, A D (2004) Automatic avoidance of obstacles is a dorsal stream function: evidence from optic ataxia. *Nature Neuroscience,* 7: 779–84.

Schneider, GE (1967) Contrasting visuomotor functions of tectum and cortex in the golden hamster. *Psychologische Forschung,* 31: 52–62.

Schneider, GE (1969) Two visual systems: brain mechanisms for localization and discrimination are dissociated by tectal and cortical lesions. *Science,* 163: 895–902.

Scoville, WB and Milner, B (1957) Loss of recent memory after bilateral hippocampal lesions. *Journal of Neurology, Neurosurgery, and Psychiatry,* 20: 11–21.

Segal, SJ and Fusella, V (1970) Influence of imaged pictures and sounds on detection of visual and auditory signals. *Journal of Experimental Psychology,* 83: 458–64.

Seidenberg, MS (1988) Cognitive neuropsychology and language: the state of the art. *Cognitive Neuropsychology,* 5: 403–26.

Seidenberg, MS and McClelland, JL (1989) A distributed, developmental model of word recognition and naming. *Psychological Review,* 96: 523–68.

Selfridge, OG (1959) Pandemonium: a paradigm for learning, in Blake, D and Uttley, A (eds) *Mechanisation of thought processes: proceedings of a symposium held at the National Physics Laboratory* (511–29). London: HMSO.

Shaffer, LH (1975) Multiple attention in continuous verbal tasks, in Rabbitt, PMA and Dornic, S (eds) *Attention and performance* (205–13). New York: Academic Press.

Shallice, T (1979) Case study approach in neuropsychological research. *Journal of Clinical Neuropsychology,* 1: 18–-211.

Shanks, DR and St John, MF (1994) Characteristics of dissociable human learning systems. *Behavioral and Brain Sciences,* 17: 367–447.

Shiffrin, RM and Schneider, W (1977) Controlled and automatic human information processing: II. Perceptual learning, automatic attending and a general theory. *Psychological Review,* 84: 127–90.

Sidman M, Stoddard LT and Mohr JP (1968). Some additional quantitative observations of immediate memory in a patient with bilateral hippocampal lesions. *Neuropsychologia,* 6: 245–54.

Smith, DJ and Minda, JP (2000) Thirty categorization results in search of a model. *Journal of Experimental Psychology: Learning, Memory, and Cognition,* 26: 3–27.

Smith, SM and Vela, E (2001) Environmental context-dependent memory: a review and meta-analysis. *Psychonomic Bulletin and Review,* 8: 203–20.

Smith, TS, Isaak, MI, Senette, CG and Abadie, BG (2011) Effects of cell-phone and text-message distractions on true and false recognition. *Cyberpsychology, Behavior, and Social Networking,* 14: 351–58.

Spelke, ES, Hirst, WC and Neisser, U (1976) Skills of divided attention. *Cognition,* 4: 215–30.

Sperling, G (1960) The information that is available in brief visual presentations. *Psychological Monographs,* 74: 1–29.

Squire, LR (1992) Declarative and nondeclarative memory: multiple brain systems supporting learning and memory. *Journal of Cognitive Neuroscience,* 4: 232–43.

Staub, A, Rayner, K, Pollatsek, A, Hyönä, J, and Majewski, H (2007) The time course of plausibility effects on eye movements in reading: evidence from noun-noun compounds. *Journal of Experimental Psychology: Learning, Memory, and Cognition,* 33: 1162–69.

Staub, A, White, SJ, Drieghe, D, Hollway, EC and Rayner, K (2010). Distributional effects of word frequency on eye fixation durations. *Journal of Experimental Psychology: Human Perception and Performance,* 36: 1280–93.

Stoerig, P and Cowey, A (1992) Wavelength discrimination in blindsight. *Brain,* 115: 425–44.

Sullivan, L (1976) Selective attention and secondary message analysis: a reconsideration of Broadbent's filter model of selective attention. *The Quarterly Journal of Experimental Psychology,* 28: 167–78.

Sutcliffe, JP (1993) Concept, class, and category in the tradition of Aristotle, in Van Mechelen, I, Hampton, J, Michalski, RS and Theuns, P (eds) *Categories and concepts: theoretical views and inductive data analysis* (35–65). San Diego, CA: Academic Press.

Swets, B, Desmet, T, Clifton, C and Ferreira, F (2008) Underspecification of syntactic ambiguities: evidence from self-paced reading. *Memory & Cognition,* 36: 201–16.

Tanenhaus, MK, Spivey-Knowlton, MJ, Eberhard, KM and Sedivy, JC (1995) Integration of visual and linguistic information in spoken language comprehension. *Science,* 268: 1632–34.

Teuber, H (1955) Physiological psychology. *Annual Review of Psychology,* 6: 267–96.

Thomas, JC (1974) An analysis of behaviour in the hobbits-orcs problem. *Cognitive Psychology,* 6: 257–69.

Treisman, AM (1960) Contextual cues in selective listening. *Quarterly Journal of Experimental Psychology,* 12: 242–48.

Treisman, AM (1964) Monitoring and storage of irrelevant messages. *Journal of Verbal Learning and Verbal Behavior,* 3: 449–59.

Trevethan, CT, Sahraie, A and Weiskrantz, L (2007) Can blindsight be superior to 'sighted-sight'? *Cognition,* 103: 491–501.

Trueswell, JC (1996) The role of lexical frequency in syntactic ambiguity resolution. *Journal of Memory and Language,* 35: 566–85.

Trueswell, JC, Tanenhaus, MK and Garnsey, SM (1994) Semantic influences on parsing: use of thematic role information in syntactic ambiguity resolution. *Journal of Memory and Language,* 33: 285–318.

Tulving, E (1972) Episodic and semantic memory, in Tulving, E and Donaldson, W (eds) *Organisation of memory.* New York: Academic Press.

Tulving, E and Osler, S (1968) Effectiveness of retrieval cues in memory for words. *Journal of Experimental Psychology,* 77: 593–601.

Tversky, A and Kahneman, D (1973) Availability: a heuristic for judging frequency and probability. *Cognitive Psychology,* 5: 207–32.

Tversky, A and Kahneman, D (1981) The framing of decisions and the psychology of choice. *Science,* 211: 453–58.

Tyler, LK and Marslen-Wilson, WD (1977) The on-line effects of semantic context on syntactic processing. *Journal of Verbal Learning and Verbal Behavior,* 16: 645–59.

Ullman, S (1998) Three-dimensional object recognition based on the combination of views. *Cognition,* 67: 21–44.

Underwood, BJ (1957) Interference and forgetting. *Psychological Review,* 64: 49–60.

Ungerleider, LG and Mishkin, M (1982) Two cortical visual systems, in Ingle, DJ, Goodale, MA and Mansfield, RJW (eds) *Analysis of visual behaviour.* Cambridge, MA: MIT Press.

Unsworth, N and Brewer, GA (2010) Individual differences in false recall: a latent variable analysis. *Journal of Memory and Language,* 62: 19–34.

Van Paemel, W and Storms, G (2008) In search of abstraction: the varying abstraction model of categorization. *Psychonomic Bulletin and Review,* 15: 732–49.

Velmans, M (2009) How to define consciousness: and how not to define consciousness. *Journal of Consciousness Studies,* 16: 139–56.

Vighetto, A (1980) Etude neuropsychologique et psychophysique de lataxie optique. Thèse Université Claude Bernard Lyon I.

Von Neumann, J and Morgenstern, O (1947) *The theory of games and economic behavior.* 2nd edition. Princeton, NJ: Princeton University Press.

Warren, P (1996) Prosody and parsing: an introduction. *Language and Cognitive Processes,* 11: 1–16.

Warren, T and McConnell, K (2007) Investigating effects of selectional restriction violations and plausibility violation severity on eye-movements in reading. *Psychonomic Bulletin & Review,* 14: 770–75.

Warrington, EK (1981) Concrete word dyslexia. *British Journal of Psychology,* 72: 175–96.

Weiskrantz, L (1998) *Blindsight: a case study and implications,* 2nd edition. Oxford: Oxford University Press.

Weiskrantz, L, Warrington, EK, Sanders, MD and Marshall, J (1974) Visual capacity in the hemianopic field following a restricted occipital ablation. *Brain,* 97: 709–28.

Wertheimer, M (1923). Untersuchugen zur Lehre von der Gestalt, II. *Psychologische Forschung, 4:* 301–50. [Laws of organisation in perceptual forms] Excerpts translated and reprinted in Ellis, WD (ed.) *A source book of Gestalt psychology* (71–80). New York: Routledge.

Whaley, CP (1978) Word-nonword classification time. *Journal of Verbal Learning and Verbal Behavior,* 17: 143–54.

Wickelgren, WA (1968) Unidimensional strength theory and component analysis of noise in absolute and comparative judgements. *Journal of Mathematical Psychology,* 5: 102–22.

Wickens, CD (1984) Processing resources in attention, in Parasuraman, R and Davies, R (eds) *Varieties of attention* (63–101). New York: Academic Press.

Wiley, J (1998) Expertise as mental set: the effects of domain knowledge in creative problem solving. *Memory & Cognition,* 26: 716–30.

Wilford, MM and Wells, GL (2010) Does facial processing prioritize change detection? Change blindness illustrates costs and benefits of holistic processing. *Psychological Science,* 21: 1611–15.

Wixted, JT (2004) The psychology and neuroscience of forgetting. *Annual Review of Psychology,* 55: 235–69.

Yarkoni, T, Balota, D and Yap, M (2008) Moving beyond Coltheart's N: a new measure of orthographic similarity. *Psychonomic Bulletin & Review,* 15: 971–79.

Yates, M, Locker, L and Simpson, GB (2004) The influence of phonological neighborhood on visual word perception. *Psychonomic Bulletin & Review,* 11: 452–57.

Zadeh, LA (1965) Fuzzy sets. *Information and Control,* 8: 338–53.

Index